ROSSICA 22

INTERNATIONAL REVIEW OF RUSSIAN CULTURE

ROSSICA 22 is the second issue in 'A New Chapter', a special double release marking the Russian Market Focus at the London Book Fair, bringing the best in contemporary Russian literature to an English-speaking audience. ROSSICA 22 showcases the diversity and quality of Russian fiction: featured extracts range from the intellectual games of Evgeny Vodolazkin's quasi-academic 'research novel' Solovyov and Larionov to the hard-boiled police procedural of Alexandra Marinina's taut crime thriller The City Rate; from the nineteenth-century realia of Pavel Basinsky's Escape from Paradise, his best-selling life of Tolstoy, to Anna Starobinets' vivid vision of the future, The Living One. As if this were not enough, this issue also boasts new translations of the latest works by two of the established stars of the Russian literary scene – Mikhail Shishkin and Dina Rubina.

This year marks the fiftieth anniversary of the first manned space flight by Yuri Gagarin on 12 April 1961. It is, therefore, very fitting that this issue of ROSSICA includes an exclusive preview of Lev Danilkin's forthcoming biography of Gagarin which describes the cosmonaut's historic visit to Britain later in the same year.

We would like to thank the huge number of people involved in the production of these two volumes: literary agents, publishers, translators, designers and many more. ROSSICA is reliant on their co-operation, and their dedication to sharing Russia's literary treasures with the world.

Svetlana A. Adjoubei
Director, Academia Rossica

A NEW CHAPTER PART 2

RUSSIAN WRITING FROM THE 21ST CENTURY

MIKHAIL SHISHKIN
LETTER BOOK
(EXTRACT)

Translated by Andrew Bromfield

I open yesterday's *Evening News*, and it's all about you and me.

It's going to be the word in the beginning again, they write. But meanwhile in the schools they rattle on in the same old way, saying first of all there was a big bang, and the whole of existence went flying apart.

And what's more, supposedly everything already existed before the bang – all the words that still hadn't been said, all the galaxies we can see and the ones we can't. In the same way that the future glass lives in the sand, and the grains of sand are the seeds of this window here, through which I've just seen a little boy run past outside with a football stuffed up the front of his tee-shirt.

There was this bundle of intense warmth and light.

And the scientists tell us it was the size of a football. Or a watermelon. And just like in the old riddle about the room full of people, with no doors or windows, we were tiny little seeds inside it. And when everything there inside was ripe and ready, it strained with all its might and burst out.

The primal watermelon hatched.

The seeds went flying off and sprouted.

One little seed put out a shoot and became our tree: there's the shadow of one of its branches, creeping along the windowsill.

Another became the memory of a girl who wanted to be a boy – once when she was still little they dressed her up as Puss-in-Boots for a fancy dress party, and everyone there kept trying to pull her tail, and in the end they tore it right off and she had to walk around with her tail in her hand.

A third little seed sprouted many years ago and became a young man who liked me to scratch his back, and hated lies, especially when they started shouting from all the pulpits that there was no death, that words written down were a kind of tram that carried you off into immortality.

In the Druidic horoscope he was a Carrot.

Before he burned his diary and all his manuscripts, he wrote one final phrase, a terribly funny one: "The gift has abandoned me" – I managed to read it before you tore that notebook out of my hands.

We stood by the bonfire and held our open hands up to our faces to block the heat, looking at the bones of our fingers showing through the transparent red flesh. Flakes of ash showered down on us – the warm, burnt-up pages.

Ah yes, I almost forgot, and afterwards the whole of existence will gather itself back into a single full stop.

Where are you now, Vovka the Carrot?

And now what's going on? Silly little Julie tries so hard, sending him letters, but hard-hearted Saint-Preux fobs her off with facetious little missives, sometimes in verse, rhyming Swedes and centipedes, ammunition and sublimation, shithouse and Mona Lisa (by the way, have you guessed what she's smiling at? – I think I have), navel and God.

My love!

Why did you do that?

* * *

The only thing still left to do was to choose myself a war. But naturally, that was no great obstacle. If there's one thing that's meat and drink to this unbeaten homeland of ours, that's it – you can't even get the newspaper open properly before friendly kingdoms are spiking little infants on their bayonets and raping old women. Somehow you feel especially sorry for the innocent tsarevich murdered in his sailor suit. The women, old men and children just seem to slip in one ear and out the other, as usual, but that sailor suit ...

A rousing tattoo on a tin drum, a murky pall hanging over the bell tower, your motherland is calling you!

At the conscription centre the prescription was: Everyone needs his own Austerlitz!

Oh, indeed he does.

At the medical board the army doctor – a huge cranium, bald and knobbly – looked into my eyes intently. He said:

"You despise everybody. You know, I used to be like that too. I was the same age as you when I did my first hospital internship. And one day they brought in a street bum who'd been knocked down by a car. He was still alive, but he'd been maimed very badly. We didn't really make much of an effort. It was obvious no one wanted the old man and no one was going to come for him. Stench, filth, lice, pus. Anyway, we put him on one side, where he wouldn't pollute anything. He was a goner in any case. And when he was gone, I was supposed to tidy up, wash the body and despatch it to the morgue. Everybody went away and left me on my own. I went out for a smoke and I thought: What do I want with this hassle? What's this old man to me? What's he good for? While I was smoking, he passed on. So there I am, wiping off the blood and pus – working sloppily, doing just enough to shunt him off to the freezer as quick as possible. And then suddenly I thought he could be somebody's father. I brought a basin of hot water and started bathing him. An old body, neglected and pitiful. Nobody had caressed it in years. And there I am washing his feet, his gruesome gnarled toes, and there are almost no nails – they've all been eaten away by fungus. I sponge down all his wounds and scars, and I talk to him quietly: Well then, dad, life turned out hard for you, did it? It's not easy when no one loves you. And what were you thinking, at your age, living out on the street, like a stray dog? But it's all over and done with now. You rest! Everything's all right now. Nothing hurts, no one's chasing after you. So I washed him and talked to him like that. I don't know if it helped him in his death, but it certainly helped me a lot to live.

My Sashenka!

* * *

Volodenka!

I watch the sunset. And I think: What if right now, this very moment, you're watching this sunset too? And that means we're together.

It's so quiet all around.

And what a sky!

That elder tree over there – even it senses the world around it.

At moments like this, the trees seem to understand everything, only they can't say it – exactly like us.

And suddenly I feel very intensely that thoughts and words are really made out of the same essence as this glow, or this glow reflected in the puddle over there, or my hand with the bandaged thumb. How I want you to see all of this!

Just imagine, I took the bread knife and somehow managed to slice my thumb right through to the nail. I bandaged it up sloppily, and then drew two eyes and a nose on the bandage. And I had a little Tom Thumb. So I've been talking to him about you all evening.

I reread your first postcard. Yes! Yes! Yes! That's it exactly! Everything rhymes! Take a look around! It's all rhymes! There's the visible world, and there – if you close your eyes – is the invisible one. There's the branch of a pine tree darning the sky, and there's its rhyme – a conch that has become an ashtray in mundane reality. There's the clock on the wall and there on the shelf is a clump of herbs from the pharmacy for relieving wind. This is my bandaged thumb – the scar will probably stay forever now – and the rhyme to it is the same thumb, but before I was born and after I've gone, which is probably the same thing. Everything in the world is rhymed with everything in the world. These rhymes connect up the world, hold it together, like nails pounded in right up to the head, to stop it falling apart.

And the most amazing thing is that these rhymes already existed in the beginning – it's not possible to invent them, just as it's impossible to invent the very simplest mosquito or that long-distance cloud over there. You understand, no amount of imagination would be enough to invent the very simplest things!

Who was it that wrote about people greedy for happiness? How well put! That's me – greedy for happiness.

And I've started noticing myself repeating your gestures, too. I speak in your words. I look with your eyes. I think like you. I write like you.

All the time I remember our summer.

Our morning studies in oil, painted with butter on toast.

Do you remember our table under the lilac, covered with the plastic tablecloth with a brown triangle from a hot iron?

And here's something you can't remember, it's mine alone: when you walked across the grass in the morning, you seemed to leave a glittering ski-track in the sun.

And the smells from the garden! So rich and dense, like fine particles saturating the air. You could pour those smells into a cup like strong tea.

And everything all around has only one thing on its mind – I simply walk through the field or the forest and everyone tries his very best to pollinate me or inseminate me. My socks are just covered in grass seeds.

And remember, we found a hare in the grass with its legs cut off by a mowing machine.

Brown-eyed cows.

Little goat nuts lying on the path.

Our pond – murky on the bottom with blooming slush, full of frogspawn. Silver carp butting at the sky. I climb out of the water and pluck the weed off myself.

I lay down to sunbathe and covered my face with my singlet, the wind rustles like starched linen. And suddenly there's a ticklish feeling in my navel, and it's you pouring a thin stream of sand onto my stomach out of your fist.

We walk home and the wind tests the trees and us to see what kind of sails we would make.

We collect fallen apples – the first ones, sour, good for compote – and we throw these windfalls at each other.

At sunset the forest is jagged.

And in the middle of the night a mousetrap jumps with a snap and wakes us up.

* * *

Sashenka, my dearest!

Well then, I'll number my letters to know which one has gone missing.

I'm sorry my scribblings turn out so short – I have absolutely no time for myself. And I'm terribly short of sleep, I feel like closing my eyes and falling asleep standing up. Descartes was killed by having to get up at five in the morning, when it was still dark, to give lectures on philosophy to Christina, Queen of Sweden. But I'm still holding on.

I was in the general staff office today and I suddenly saw my reflection in a mirror, in full dress uniform. It was strange, what was I doing in fancy dress? I was amazed at myself: how could I be a soldier?

You know, there's something to this life after all, always covering off in line with the cheekbone of the fourth man.

I'll tell you a story about a forage cap. It's a short one. It was filched from me – the forage cap, that is. And falling in without a forage cap is a breach of regulations, in short, it's a crime.

Our chief of chiefs and commander of commanders stamped his feet and promised me I'd be washing out the shithouse from now until doomsday.

"You'll lick it out, you scumbag!"

That's what he said.

Well now, there is something inspiring about military speech. I read somewhere that Stendhal learned to write simply and clearly by studying Napoleon's field orders.

But the latrine here, my dear, distant Sashenka, requires some explanation. Picture to yourself holes in a floor covered with filth. No, better not picture it! And everyone tries his very best to dump his heap on the edge of a hole, not in it. And everything's awash. Actually, the way the stomachs of yours truly and his fellows function is a separate subject in its own right. In these remote parts, for some reason we always have a bellyache. I don't understand how you can dedicate yourself to Generalissimus Suvorov's science of victory if you're always squatting over a yawning abyss with your insides draining out of you.

Anyway, I say to him:

"Where will I get a forage cap for you?"

And he says:

"They filched yours, you go and filch one!"

So off I went to filch a forage cap. And that's not easy. In fact, it's very hard, because everyone's at it.

There I was, wandering hither and thither.

And I suddenly thought: Who am I? Where am I?

And I went to wash the latrine. And the whole world suddenly seemed lighter somehow.

I had to end up here to learn to understand simple things.

You know, there's nothing dirty about shit.

* * *

Now look, I'm writing to you at night. I nibbled a crust of bread in bed just now, and the crumbs won't let me sleep, they've scampered all over the sheet and they bite.

The window above my head is as starry as starry.

And the Milky Way divides the sky on a slant. You know, it's like some gigantic fraction. The numerator is one half of the universe, and the denominator is the other half. I always hated those fractions, squared numbers, cubed numbers and all those roots. It's all so disembodied, impossible to visualise, there's absolutely nothing to grab hold of. A root is a root – on a tree. It's strong, it creeps and grabs, it gobbles the soil, it's clinging, sucking, irrepressible, greedy, alive. But this is twaddle written with a little squiggle, and they call it a root too!

And what sense does a minus sign make? Minus a window – what's that? It's not going to go anywhere. And neither is what's outside the window.

Or minus me?

Things like that don't happen.

In general, I'm the kind of person who has to touch everything.

And sniff.

Yes, even more – sniff everything. Like in the book daddy used to read to me at bedtime when I was little. There are different kinds of people. There are people who spend all their time fighting with cranes. There are people with one leg, they dash around on it at high speed, and their foot is so big that they shelter in its vast shadow from the sweltering heat of the sun and rest there, as if they were inside a house. And there's another kind of people too, who live on nothing but the smells of fruits. When they have to set out on a long journey, they take these fruits with them, and if they catch a whiff of a bad smell, they die. That's just like me.

You know, in order to exist, everything alive has to have a smell. At least some kind of smell. And all those fractions and all the other stuff we were taught – it has no smell.

There's some kind of night prowler outside the window now, kicking an empty bottle about. The clink of glass on the asphalt of a deserted street.

Now it's broken.

At moments like this at night I feel so lonely and I want so much to be the reason for at least something.

And I long unbearably to be with you! To hug you and snuggle up against you.

Do you know what you'll get if you divide that starry numerator by the denominator? Divide one half of the Universe by the other? You'll get me. And you with me.

Today I saw a little girl fall off her bike – she skinned her knee and sat there crying bitterly, and her long white sock was splattered with blood. It was on the embankment, where the lions are – mouths stuffed full of litter, paper wrappers and sticks from ice cream. Then afterwards I was walking home and suddenly the idea came to me that all the great books and pictures aren't about love at all. They only pretend to be about love, so they'll be interesting to read. But in actual fact, they're about death. In books, love is a kind of shield or, rather, a blindfold. So you don't see. So it's not so frightening.

I don't know what the connection was with that little girl who fell off her bike.

She cried a bit, and now perhaps she's forgotten about it ages ago, but in a book her skinned knee would have stayed there until she died and even afterwards.

Probably all books aren't really about death, but about eternity, only their eternity isn't genuine, it's a kind of fragment, an instant, like a teensy-weensy fly in amber. It just sat down for a moment to rub its back legs together, and it turned out to be forever. Of course, they choose all sorts of fine moments, but isn't it a terrifying thought – to stay like that, forever porcelain – like the shepherd boy always reaching out to kiss the shepherd girl!

But I don't want anything porcelain. I want everything alive, here and now. You, your warmth, your voice, your body, your smell.

You're so far away now that I'm not at all afraid to tell you something. You know, back then at the dacha, I used to go into your room while you weren't there. And I sniffed everything. Your soap. Your eau de cologne. Your shaving brush. I sniffed the inside of your shoes. I opened your cupboard and sniffed your sweater. The sleeve of your shirt. And the collar. I kissed a button. I leaned down over your bed and put my nose to the pillow. I was so happy! But that wasn't enough! To be happy, you need witnesses. You can only really feel happy when you get some kind of confirmation, if not from a glance or a touch, or a presence, than at least from an absence. From a pillow, a sleeve, a button. Once you almost caught me – I only just managed to run out onto the porch. And you saw me and started throwing prickly burrs in my hair. I was so angry with you then, but what wouldn't I give now for that – to have you throw burrs in my hair!

I remember you, and the world is divided into before the first time and after.

Our meetings by the monument.

I peeled an orange and my palm stuck to yours.

You came straight from the clinic, with a fresh filling in your tooth and the smell of the dentist's surgery coming out of your mouth. You let me touch the filling with my finger.

And here we are at the dacha, whitewashing the ceiling, after we've covered the furniture and the floor with old newspapers. We walked around barefoot, with the newspapers sticking to our feet, and got whitewash smeared all over us. We scrape the white out of each other's hair. And our tongues and teeth are all black from bird cherries.

Then when we were hanging the net curtains up, we ended up on different sides, and I wanted so much for you to kiss me through the netting!

And then there you sit, drinking tea, burning your tongue on it and blowing to get it to cool down, taking little sips and slurping so loudly, not at all worried about it being impolite, as they impressed on me when I was little. And I start slurping too. Because I'm not little any longer. And everything's allowed.

Then there was the lake.

We walk down the steep slope towards the waterlogged bank, feeling the damp, spongy path under our bare feet.

We waded out into open water, free of duckweed. The water's murky and full of sunlight. And cold, from the springs that feed it from below.

And then, in the water, our bodies touched for the first time. On the shore I was afraid to touch you, but here I pounced on you and wrapped my legs round your thighs, trying to pull you under. When I was little I used to play like that with daddy at the seaside. You try to break free, you try to pull my hands apart, but I won't give in. I kept trying to duck your head right under the water. Your eyelashes stick together, you swallow lots of water, you laugh and splutter and bellow and snort.

Afterwards we sit in the sun.

Your nose is peeling, the skin is flaking off the sunburn.

We watch the bell tower on the opposite shore rinsing its ragged image in the water.

I sit there in front of you almost naked, but somehow I only feel shy about my feet and my toes – I buried them in the sand.

I singed an ant with my cigarette, and you came to its defence.

We walk home the short way, straight across the field. Grasshoppers jumping about in the tall grass molest my skirt.

On the veranda you sat me in a wicker chair and started brushing the sand off my feet. Like daddy. When we came back from the beach, he used to wipe my feet down just like that, so there wouldn't be any sand left between my toes.

And everything was suddenly so clear. So simple. So inevitable. So welcome.

I stand there facing you – in my wet swimsuit, with my arms lowered. I look into your eyes. You took hold of the straps and pulled the swimsuit off.

I'd been ready for this for a long time, I was waiting, but I was afraid, and you were even more afraid, and everything would have happened much sooner, but that time, back in spring, remember, I took your hand and pulled it down there, but you jerked it away. You were quite different now.

Do you know what I was afraid of? Pain? No. There wasn't any pain. And there wasn't any blood either. I thought, what if you thought you weren't my first?

It was evening before I remembered I'd forgotten to hang my swimsuit up to dry. It was lying there abandoned, clumped up, wet and cold. It smelled of pond scum.

I snuggled against you and kissed your peeling nose. There was no one in the house, but we whispered anyway. And for the first time I could look right into your eyes, without being afraid or embarrassed about anything – brown, with hazel and green flecks on the iris.

Absolutely everything suddenly changed – I could touch everything that only a moment ago was untouchable, not mine. A moment ago it was someone else's, but now it was mine, as if my body had expanded and melded with yours. And now I couldn't feel myself except through you. My skin only existed where you touched it.

That night you slept, but I couldn't. I wanted so much to cry, but I was afraid I'd wake you. I got up and went to the bathroom, and cried to my heart's content.

And in the morning, at the washbasin – a sudden surge of foolish happiness at the sight of our two toothbrushes in the same glass. Remember, back in town already – you locked yourself in the toilet, and I was walking by to the kitchen and I couldn't resist it, I squatted down by the door and started whispering into the keyhole:

"I love you!"

I whispered it really quietly. Then louder. And you didn't realise what I was whispering to you, and you muttered back:

"Just a moment, just a moment."

As if I needed the bathroom.

It's you I need, you!

And then there you are, sitting in front of the oven with a spoon in one hand and an open cookery book in the other. Something suddenly came over you – you said you'd cook everything yourself and I mustn't interfere. And I kept coming into the kitchen on purpose, as if I needed something, but really only to look at you. Remember? You were kneading minced meat, and I couldn't help myself, I stuck my hands in the saucepan too – it was so wonderful to knead that fragrant, beefy pulp together, and the mince oozed out between our fingers!

On the whole, you didn't get along too well with ladles, oven mitts and frying pans – everything came to life in your hands and tried its very best to wriggle free or pop up in the air or slither away.

I remember every single little thing.

We lay there clasped together and couldn't let go – and that semicircle my teeth left on your shoulder.

Our legs intertwine, our feet nestle against each other, sweet-talking, and our cream-slippery fingers slither into each other.

In the tram people turn to look at us: your left fist is up beside my nose, and I'm kissing the first knuckle on the forefinger – the one that's July.

On the way up to your place, the lift seems to creep along so unbearably slowly.

Your shoes under a chair, with the socks stuffed into them.

That was when you kissed me there for the first time, and I just couldn't relax. When you're growing up you know you mustn't touch that place. It's only little boys who think little girls have a secret between their legs, but that place is full of slimy discharges, noxious vapours and bacteria.

In the morning I couldn't find my knickers, they'd disappeared. I searched through everything and couldn't find them. I still think you pinched them and hid them somewhere. I left without them. I'm walking along the street, the wind's creeping up under my skirt, and I have the incredible feeling that it's you all around me.

I know I exist, but I need proofs all the time, I need to be touched. Without you I'm an empty pair of pyjamas, thrown across a chair.

My own arms and legs, my own body, have only become dear to me because of you – because you have kissed it, because you love it.

I look in the mirror and catch myself thinking: that's the one he loves, isn't it? And I like myself. But I never used to like myself before.

I close my eyes and imagine that you're here.

I can touch you and hug you.

I kiss your eyes, and suddenly my lips can see.

And I want so much, like I did then, to run the end of my tongue from one end to the other of the little seam you have down there, as if you were a bare-naked little boy who'd been stuck together out of two separate halves.

I read somewhere that the smelliest parts of the body are closest to the soul.

Now I've turned the light out so I can finally curl up into a tight little ball and fall asleep, and while I was writing to you, clouds have covered over the sky. As if someone has wiped everything off the school blackboard with a dirty rag and there's nothing left but white streaks.

I have a feeling everything's going to be all right. Destiny is just trying to frighten us, but it will preserve and protect us against genuine misfortune.

* * *

Sashka, my dear one!

I bluff and bluster, but in reality without you, without your letters, I would have died ages ago, or at least stopped being myself – I don't know which is worse.

I wrote to you about our tormentor, the one I dubbed "Commodus", after the infamously bloody son of Marcus Aurelius – the nickname has stuck, but the soldiers have shortened it to "Commode". No doubt because of his obsession with shit. Today he made a special effort to explain to me exactly how life works. I don't want to write about it. I want to forget, think about something else for a while, about Marcus Aurelius, for instance.

I don't understand what connection there can be between Marcus Aurelius, who died a million years ago, who everyone has heard about, and me, who no one has heard about, sitting here in my prickly official-issue underpants.

But on the other hand, here's what he wrote: No man is happy until he considers himself happy.

Probably that's what we have in common – we're two happy men. And what difference does it make that he died one day, and I'm still here? Compared to our happiness, death seems like a mere trifle. He stepped straight through it to me, as if it was a doorway.

This feeling of happiness comes from the realisation that none of all this around me is real. What is real is that first time I was at your place and I went into the bathroom to wash my hands and saw your sponge there and felt so intensely aware that it had touched your breasts.

My Sashenka! We were together, but I've only really begun to understand that here.

And now I remember it all and I'm astonished I didn't appreciate it all properly then.

Remember, the fuses blew at your dacha, you held the candle for me and I stood on a chair,

fiddling with my makeshift repair. I glanced at you, and you looked so incredible in the semi-darkness, with the light from the candle flame washing over your face! And the spark of the candle was reflected in your eyes.

Or look at this, we're walking through our park, and you keep running off the asphalt strip of the path, tearing up bunches of grass and bringing different kinds of seed heads to show me.

"What's this? And what's this called?"

You walk on, and your heels are smeared with mud.

Your poor toe is all blue – someone trod on it and crushed it in the tram, and you're wearing open-toed shoes.

Then I see the lake.

The water has turned thick, overgrown with duckweed and clouds.

You walked right up to the edge, lifted your skirt and stepped into the water, up to your ankles – to try it. You shouted:

"It's cold!"

You pulled one foot out and ran it across the surface, as if you were ironing out creases.

I see it all as if it was happening right now, not then.

You got undressed, tied up your long, loose hair, and you walk into the water, checking the bun on your head several times.

You turn over on your back and flail at the lake with your legs, and your heels twinkle pink in the foamy spray.

Then you throw out your arms and legs, lying there like a star, the bun on your head comes undone and your long hair spreads out in all directions.

Later, on the shore, I glanced stealthily – so you wouldn't notice – at the place between your legs where the wet curls were peeping out from under the elastic of your swimsuit.

And now I see your room.

You take off your shoes, leaning down one shoulder, then the other.

I kiss the palms of your hands, and you say:

"Don't, they're dirty!"

You clasp my neck in your arms and kiss me, biting my lips.

Suddenly you yelped.

I was really frightened.

"What's wrong?"

"You caught my hair under your elbow."

You leaned down over me, touched my eyelids and lashes with your nipple. You pulled your hair over both of us like a tent.

I pull off your knickers, they're like a child's – cream-coloured with little bows – and you help me, you raise your knees.

I kiss you on the spot where the skin is most tender and sensitive – on the inside of the thighs.

I bury my nose in the dense, warm undergrowth.

The bed creaks so desperately that we move to the floor.

You groaned under me and arched up in a bridge.

We lie there and the draught feels good on our sweaty legs.

Your back is covered with delicate fluff and patterns from the coarse ribs of the Chinese straw mat. I run my finger along your sharp vertebrae.

I take a pen off the table and start joining up the moles on your back with an inky line. It tickles you. Afterwards you twist and turn in front of the mirror, looking over your shoulder to see how it turned out. I want to wash it off, but you say:

"Leave it!"

"Are you going to walk about like that?"

"Yes."

You flung your feet up on the wall and suddenly started running across the wallpaper in little steps, you arched up, braced your elbows on the straw mat and froze with your legs up like that. I couldn't resist it, I wanted to kiss you there – you folded up straightaway, collapsed.

I'm leaving, and you've come out to show me to the door – in just a little singlet, with nothing underneath it. You suddenly start feeling embarrassed and pull down the hem at the front with your hand.

On our last night I woke up and listened to your snuffling.

You were used to sleeping like a chrysalis, you wrapped the blanket round your head and only left a little air hole for breathing. I lie there, looking into that hole. And you're so funny – you've gone to sleep with a chocolate sweet stuffed in your cheek, and there's chocolate dribbling out of your mouth.

I lie there, keeping watch over your breathing.

I listen closely to your rhythm. And I try to breath together with you. In – out , in – out. In – out.

Slowly – slowly. Like this.

In.

Out.

You know, I'd never felt so light and easy as at that moment. I looked at you, so beautiful, so serene and sleepy, I touched the hairs peeping out from your blanket cocoon, and I wanted so much to protect you from that night, from any drunken night-time yelling outside the window, from the whole world.

My Sashenka! Sleep! Sleep well! I'm here, I'm breathing with you.

In.

Out.

In.

Out.

In.

Out.

* * *

I peeped into the letter box – again nothing from you.

I have to prepare for a seminar tomorrow, and my head's empty. I don't care. I'm going to brew some coffee, pull my feet up on the armchair and talk to you right now. Listen.

Remember how good it felt telling each other things about our childhood? You know, there's so much I still haven't told you yet.

But now I'm chewing on my pen and I don't know where to start.

Do you know why I was given my name?

When I was little I adored all the lovely different little boxes and caskets in the bottom drawers of our sideboard, I spent ages rummaging through the things my mother kept there – bracelets, brooches, playing cards, post cards, everything on earth. And then in one box I found a pair of child's sandals – all tiny and shrivelled, small enough for a doll.

It turned out that I had an older brother.

When he was three, he fell ill and was taken into hospital. And what they said about him was really terrible – they said he was doctored to death.

My parents immediately decided to have another child. To take his place.

And a little girl was born. Me.

My mother couldn't accept her child, she didn't feed me and didn't want to see me. They told me all this afterwards. It was my father who pulled me through. Me and my mother.

In my baby bed three of the wooden bars had been sawn out so I could crawl through. But it was his bed, the other child's. Only I couldn't understand then that the hole was for him. That he used to crawl through it. I liked scampering through it as well, but I was really only repeating his movements.

For me that boy had been left behind in some unimaginable life before I was born. If it ever existed, then it had faded into a kind of prehistoric age, but for my mother it was right there beside me, all the time, it never went away. One day we were going to the dacha on the train and a child was sitting opposite us with his grandmother. Just a normal child with a squeaky voice and runny nose who couldn't pronounce his r's properly. He kept pestering his grandmother for something. And she kept snapping back:

"Just calm down, will you!"

And I remember the way my mother flinched and shrank when the old woman said:

"Sasha! We're getting off here!"

When we got off the train, my mother turned away and started rummaging desperately in her handbag, and I saw the tears pouring out of her eyes. I started snivelling and she turned round and kissed me with her wet lips, trying to reassure me that everything was all right, that it was just a midge that had flown into her eye.

"But everything's fine now!"

She blew her nose, touched up her mascara and snapped her powder compact shut. And off we went to the dacha.

I remember that was when I thought: It's a good thing that child died. Otherwise, where would I be now? As I walked along, I repeated what my mother had said: "But everything's fine now!"

I couldn't *not* have been born, could I? Everything around me, everything that was and is and will be, is simple and adequate proof of that, even this small window-frame with its mouth wide open, and these flat pancakes of sunshine on the floor, and the cheesy flakes of curdled milk in this mug of coffee, and this faded mirror playing at stares with the window to see who'll blink first.

As a little girl I used to spend hours gazing into the mirror. Eye to eye. Why these eyes? Why this face? Why this body?

What if it's not me? And these aren't my eyes, or my face, or my body?

What if I – with these eyes and face and body that I just glimpsed – what if all this is just a memory of some old woman I'll become some day?

Often I used to pretend there were really two of me. Like twin sisters. Me and her. Like in the fairytales: one bad and one good. Me the well-behaved one, and her the hooligan.

I used to wear my hair long, my mother was always nagging at me to comb it. And she took the scissors and snipped off my plait out of spite.

We used to have theatre shows at the dacha and, of course, she played all the leading roles, and I opened and closed the curtain. And then once, in the course of the action, she was supposed to kill herself. Just imagine it, she says her final words with a knife in her hand, then swings and hits her head as hard as she can, and suddenly she's covered in real blood. Everybody jumped to their feet in horror, and she's lying there dying – in the play, and from sheer delight as well. Only I knew that she'd grated some beetroot, taken a hen's egg and sucked it out through a little hole and used a syringe she took from mummy to squirt the juice into the egg and hidden it in her wig. She jumped up, all covered in beetroot blood, squealing in joy at having fooled everyone:

"You believed it! You believed it!"

You simply can't imagine what it's like having to put up with her all the time! You can't imagine what it's like to wear her cast-offs after she's done with them. They always bought beautiful new things for her, that princess without a pea, and I got the same things, already old and disgusting, to wear out. They deck us out for school after the summer holidays, and she has nice new shoes, but I have to get into her old raincoat with holes in the pockets and a stain on the lapel.

She tormented me all my childhood, whenever the fancy took her. I remember I drew a white chalk boundary line on the floor, divided our room in half. She went and rubbed it out and drew the line so that I could only walk round the edge from my bed to the table and the door. It was pointless complaining to mummy, because with mummy she was an absolute angel, but when we were left alone, she started pinching me and pulling my hair until it really hurt, so that I wouldn't snitch on her.

I'll never forget the time I was given a wonderful doll, a huge talking doll that closed and opened it eyes and could even walk. Just as soon as I turned away for a moment, my tormentor stripped her naked, saw there was something missing, and drew it on. I started crying and went running to my parents – they just laughed.

It was impossible to come to terms with her! I suggest something, and she stamps her little foot and declares:

"Things will be the way I say round here, or else there won't be anything at all!"

Her eyes narrow, looking daggers at me, and her upper lip twitches too, exposing her sharp little teeth. She's going to grab me any moment…

I remember how scared I was when mummy asked me who I was talking to. I lied:

"Myself."

I realise that it used to happen when I wanted to be loved. She appeared when I had to fight for other people's love. That is, almost all the time – even when I was on my own. But never with daddy. With daddy everything was different.

He called mummy and me the same name – we were both bunnies. He probably enjoyed shouting: "Bunny!" – and we would both answer, one from the kitchen and one from the nursery.

When he came home, in order not to let any strangers in, before I opened the door I had to ask:

"Who's there?"

He used to answer: "A sewer and mower and tin-whistle blower".

Even when he wiped his feet on the mat in the hallway it came out like a dance.

He liked to bring me strange presents. He used to say:

"Guess what!"

But it was absolutely impossible to guess. It could be a fan, or a tea bowl, or a lorgnette, a tea caddy, an empty scent bottle or a broken camera. Once he brought a Japanese Noh Theatre mask. He even brought home a genuine elephant's foot from somewhere, hollowed out for umbrellas and canes. Mummy used to rant at him, but his presents made me feel absolutely happy.

He could suddenly say, out of the blue:

"Forget that homework!"

And then we would put on a concert. We loved humming on combs wrapped in tissue paper – it tickled my lips terribly. An empty cake box became a tambourine. He used to turn up the corner of the carpet and rattle out a tap dance on the floor, until the neighbours started banging. Or grab the box of chess pieces and start shaking it rhythmically, so that everything inside it rattled about.

He made me play chess with him and he always won, and when he got me in checkmate, he was as delighted as a little child.

He knew all the dances in the world and he taught me to dance. I don't know why, but I really loved the Hawaiian dance – we used to keep our hands in our pockets when we did it.

One day at the table he told me to stop being so silly and stubborn or he'd pour a glass of kefir over my head.

I said:

"No you won't!"

And suddenly I was covered in white kefir goo. Mummy was horrified, but I was cock-a-hoop.

I never had to fight for his love.

But when daddy wasn't there, that other me persecuted me incessantly.

I always suffered agonies with my skin, but hers was smooth and clear. Skin isn't just a sack for your insides, it's what the world uses to touch us. The world's feeler. And skin problems are just a way of protecting yourself from being touched. You sit there, hidden away, like inside a cocoon. But she – the other me – didn't understand any of this. She didn't understand that I was afraid of everything, and above all of being with other people. She didn't understand how, when we went visiting and everybody was enjoying themselves, I could lock myself in the toilet and just sit there without even taking my knickers off. She didn't understand how I could learn the theorems of Pythagoras off by heart, but freeze up in terror beside the blackboard, leave my body and float round in the air, watching myself from the outside – helpless, pitiful, desolated. The only fact about Pythagoras that remained in my head was how when he was a child and his parents showed him the basic forms through which the invisible manifests itself to human beings on a little table – globe, pyramid, cube, scraps of wool, apples, honey cakes and a little pitcher of wine – and named them all, Pythagoras listened to their explanations and then knocked the table over.

I always wrote her compositions for her. And I always got a "D". And even worse, the teacher used to read them out in class and sigh:

"Sashenka, life is going to be hard for you."

And she gave me a D, because I always wrote about the wrong thing. They gave us three subjects to choose from, we had to write about the first one, the second one or the third one – but I always wrote about God knows what. God knows what was more important to me.

I was a monster from a species of gill-winged, brachiopod moss animals. But she was the Dance of Mahanaim, with eyes like the pools in Heshbon, by the gate of *Bath-rabbim*. I remember how shocked I was by the way our PT teacher looked at her during class.

One day I was getting changed after school and I noticed someone spying on me through binoculars from behind the curtain in a window of the house opposite. I squatted down below the windowsill in horror, but she started putting on a full-scale performance.

When I was little, to frighten me at night she used to tell me she was a witch and she had power over people. And her proof for that was her eyes – the left one was blue, and the right one was brown. And she told me she used to have warts, and when we stayed the night at someone else's place, she washed herself with the sponge

in that house, and her warts disappeared, but they appeared on the child who lived there. But the main argument, of course, was her eyes. She told me she could put the evil eye on anyone she wanted. The other girls weren't exactly afraid of her, but that didn't mean much. She could definitely charm blood – she only had to lick a cut and whisper something, and the bleeding stopped.

Even now she won't leave me in peace. And you can never tell when she'll appear again. She can disappear and be gone for months, then suddenly – Here I am, surprise, surprise!

She mocks me because in the library, out of pity for the dead authors nobody wants, I take the longest-neglected books – otherwise no one will even remember about these writers. Such a slovenly trollop, she says, but you underline the ideas you like so neatly with a comb. She strikes a pose and lectures me, like an older sister: You can't live your life like a wishy-washy dishrag, you have to learn to be pushier than a lamb and louder than a mouse. Remember the seventeenth rule of Thales of Miletus, my little sister: It is better to arouse envy than pity!

And how viciously she used to tease you!

Remember, we were sitting on the veranda, eating strawberries – sour and unappetising, we were dipping them in sugar. And she got the idea of dipping them in honey. She pours some honey out of the jar into her saucer and licks the spoon. And she looks at you. And checks her expression in the mirror. I know that expression only too well, with the gleeful malice blazing in that odd pair of eyes.

She licked the spoon, took the end of it between her finger and thumb and flung it through the open veranda window behind her.

And she looks at you.

"Fetch!"

I tried to shout out to you: "Stop! Don't you dare do that!" And I couldn't force out a single word.

You got up and went to look for the spoon – and there were thickets of brambles and wild raspberry bushes out there. You came back all scratched, with beads of blood on your hands. Without saying a word, you put the spoon on the table – with the earth and dry grass sticking to it – and turned and walked away.

She simply pulled a wry face at the dirty spoon. Then, as if nothing has happened, she carries on dipping strawberries in honey and biting them with her little teeth.

I couldn't stand it, I dashed after you, grabbed hold of your arm, tried to lick your scratch the way she did, to stop the bleeding, but you shoved me away.

"Go to hell!"

And you looked at me with such contempt.

You got on your bike and rode off.

How I hated you then!

That is, I hated her.

Both of you!

And I really, really wanted something to happen to you, something bad, terrible, evil.

I told myself I wouldn't go to you

And I went running to you the very next day.

I see it all again, as if it's happening right now, feel it on my skin: It's been drizzling since morning, the mist has clambered up the fence, all the paths are drowned in puddles. I'm walking to your place with an umbrella over my head, and on the bridge over the ravine the rain starts coming down even harder.

There's a small stretch of forest between our dachas, all the footpaths there have dissolved into mud, and all the greenery sprouting there is nameless – it was only you who gave the plants their names.

I walk past your neighbours on the corner, peep over the fence at the roses – huge and heavy, like heads of cabbage. They're even more fragrant in the rain.

I felt afraid to walk up the steps onto the porch, I folded the umbrella and sneaked across to the veranda windows. I went up on tiptoe and saw you there inside the rainy windows. You're lying on the divan, with your bandaged foot up on its back, reading some thick volume

You see, I wished you ill, and you fell off your bike into the ditch.

Now you know why you twisted your ankle that evening and ended up lounging about in bed.

I stood there in the rain and looked at you. You sensed something, looked up, saw me, smiled.

PAVEL BASINSKY
LEV TOLSTOY: FLIGHT FROM PARADISE (EXTRACT)

Translated by Catherine Porter

'We all put on a brave face with each other, and forget that without love we're the most wretched of the wretched. But we grow used to acting this way and become spiteful and proud, and mistake sick chickens for fierce lions.'
Letter from Tolstoy to his friend Vladimir Chertkov

DEPARTURE OR ESCAPE?

On October 28th 1910, in the Krapivo district of Tula province, an extraordinary event occurred, even for such an extraordinary place as Yasnaya Polyana, the estate of Count Lev Nikolaevich Tolstoy: the 82-year-old writer left home in the early hours of the morning for an unknown destination, accompanied by his personal physician, Doctor Dushan Makovitsky.

What the newspapers said

The news spread quickly across Russia and the world, and by October 29th the St Petersburg Telegraph Agency was buzzing with telegrams from Tula, published the following day in the newspapers. "Shocking news of L.N. Tolstoy's departure from Yasnaya Polyana with Doctor Makovitsky. On leaving, he wrote a letter explaining that he had left for good."

Even Tolstoy's friend Makovitsky knew nothing of this letter he had written for his sleeping wife, given to her the next morning by their youngest daughter Sasha, and he learnt of it only from the newspapers.

The most detailed of these was Moscow's "Russian Word", with a report on October 30th from its special Tula correspondent:

"Tula, 29.10. Urgent. Having returned from Yasnaya Polyana, I can now confirm that Lev Nikolaevich left yesterday at five in the morning, when it was still dark. He went to the stables, having packed some essential things in the night, and ordered the horses to be harnessed. The coachman Andrian obeyed, and when the horses were ready Lev Nikolaevich drove off with Doctor Makovitsky to the station at Shchokina. Filka the groom rode ahead, lighting their way with a torch. At Shchokina, Lev Nikolaevich bought a ticket to one of the stations on the Moscow-Kursk line, and boarded the first train that arrived.

"When his departure was discovered at Yasnaya Polyana in the morning, the house was in turmoil. The despair of his wife, Sofia Andreevna, cannot be described."

This report, which the whole world was discussing the following day, was published on the third page. The front page was taken up as usual with advertisements for various products: "Saint Raphael Wine, the stomach's best friend." "Medium-sized sturgeon, 20 kopecks a pound."

On receiving the news from Tula, the paper immediately sent its correspondent to the Tolstoys' house in Moscow on Khamovniki Street, now the Tolstoy Museum, thinking he might have gone there. But according to the paper, "the Tolstoys' ancient residence was quiet, with nothing to indicate that Lev Nikolaevich was at home. The gates were locked; everyone was asleep."

A young journalist and theatre critic on the paper, Konstantin Orlov, was sent to track the runaway down. The son of one of Tolstoy's followers and a former revolutionary, depicted in his stories "The Dream" and "There Are No Guilty Men in The World," Orlov caught up with him at the station of Kozelsk, and quietly accompanied him to the remote country station of Astapovo, from where he sent Sofia Andreevna and her children a telegram informing them that he was lying gravely ill in the house of the stationmaster, I.I. Ozolin.

If it wasn't for Orlov, his family would only have learnt where he was and that he was fatally ill from the newspapers, which would have added cruelly to their distress. This was why, unlike Makovitsky, who regarded "Russian Word" as "spying", the Tolstoys' eldest daughter Tatyana described in her memoirs her "eternal gratitude" to Orlov: "Father is dying somewhere not far from here, but I don't know where, and I can't look after him. Perhaps I shall never see him again. Will they at least let me see him on his deathbed? A sleepless night. Torture," she wrote of her mental state after his "escape" (her word). "But this man we didn't know took pity on his family, and telegraphed us: 'Lev Nikolaevich in stationmaster's house in Astapovo. Temperature 40 deg'". The press was generally more tactful and restrained with his family, particularly Sofia

Andreevna, than it was with Tolstoy himself, whose every step was relentlessly pursued, despite the fact that in his farewell letter to his wife he had begged people not to look for him: "Please do not follow me, even if you learn where I am."

"At Belyovo station Lev Nikolaevich got out and ate a fried egg at the cafe," a journalist wrote, relishing the vegetarian Tolstoy's modest meal. The coachman and Filka were questioned, and the servants and peasants at Yasnaya Polyana, the buffet attendants and ticket clerks, the driver who drove him from Kozelsk to the Optina Pustyn Monastery, the monks who ran the guest-house there, and anyone who might have information about the journey of this old man, whose only wish had been to escape and hide from the world.

"Don't look for him! He's not yours, he belongs to all of us!" "Odessa News" cynically exhorted his family.

"Naturally his location will soon be discovered," coldly announced the "St Petersburg Paper".

Although he read the newspapers, Tolstoy had never disguised his dislike of them. Sofia Andreevna was another matter. She knew that like it or not his reputation and her own were formed by them, and she was happy to talk to journalists and give interviews, in which she explained this or that oddity of her husband's behaviour, never missing the chance (for this was her weakness) to emphasise her own role in the great writer's life. For this reason the media's attitude to her then was mainly sympathetic. The general tone is exemplified by the vignette "Sofia Andreevna", published on October 31 in "Russian Word", by the journalist Vlas Doroshevich. "The old lion has left to die in solitude," he wrote, and compared Sofia to Yasodhara, the wife of the Buddha. This was clearly meant as a compliment, since no one has ever blamed Yasodhara for her husband's decision to leave. More spiteful tongues however would compare Sofia to Xanthippe, the wife of Socrates, who had tormented her husband with her shrewish behaviour and hostility to his ideas.

Doroshevich correctly pointed out that Tolstoy wouldn't have lived for so long or written his late works without her (although it's not clear what this has to do with Yasodhara), but the article's conclusion was that the writer was "superhuman", and couldn't be judged by normal human rules. As a simple earthly woman, Sofia Andreevna did everything she could for her husband as a man, but the "superhuman" aspects of his life were inaccessible to her, and this was her tragedy. Sofia read the piece and liked it. She was grateful for Doroshevich's article, and for Orlov's telegram, and she turned a blind eye to details such as Orlov's unflattering depiction of her: "Sofia Andreevna's head was shaking, and her eyes wandered, expressing her inner torment. She was shabbily dressed in an old housecoat." She could even forgive the journalists who stalked the house in Moscow, and tasteless references to the sum she later paid for a special train to take the family from Tula to Astapovo (492 roubles 27 kopecks), and the literary critic Vasily Rozanov's transparent reference to Tolstoy escaping from his family ("the prisoner breaking free of his jail.")

The headlines at the time spoke not of his "departure", but of "SUDDEN FLIGHT", "DISAPPEARANCE", and in English, "TOLSTOY QUITS HOME." This wasn't from any desire to sensationalise the affair, it was sensational enough as it was, but because the circumstances of his leaving were more reminiscent of escape than a triumphant departure.

The nightmare

He left at night, while the Countess was asleep, and had taken such pains to keep it secret from her that the first she knew of his whereabouts was on November 2nd, from Orlov's telegram. Yet what neither she nor the journalists knew was that he himself had no clear idea of his itinerary when he left, still less his final destination.

In the first hours of his departure, only his daughter Sasha and her companion Varvara Feokritova knew that he planned to visit his sister Maria the nun in her convent at Shamordino. But even on the night itself he was having second thoughts about this, as Sasha recalled in her memoirs: "'You stay here, Sasha,' he said. 'I'll send for you in a couple of days when I've decided definitely where I'm going. I'll probably go to Mashenka's in Shamordino.'"

He told Doctor Makovitsky nothing of this when he woke him in the night. More importantly, he didn't tell the doctor he was leaving Yasnaya Polyana for good, as he had told Sasha, and for the first few hours Makovitsky assumed they were going to Kochety, the estate of his daughter Tatyana and her husband Mikhail Sukhotin, on the border between Tula and Orlov provinces. Tolstoy had paid several visits there in the past two years, on his own and with his wife, to escape the flood of visitors at Yasnaya, and there he could take a "holiday", as he put it. Unlike Sasha, Tatyana didn't approve of his desire to leave her mother, even though she took his side in the conflicts between them. But he knew he couldn't hide from Sofia Andreevna in Kochety. His plan to visit Shamordino was less calculated. The excommunicated Tolstoy's appearance in an Orthodox convent would be an event no less scandalous than his flight, but he knew he could count on his sister and her support and discretion.

Poor Makovitsky, thinking they had left to stay in Kochety for a month, had taken almost no money with him, and didn't know that Tolstoy's only funds were 50 rouble notes in a notebook and some loose change in his wallet. It was only as Tolstoy was saying goodbye to Sasha that he heard Shamordino mentioned, and he noted later in his diary that as they set off in the carriage he had asked his advice, and his words "How far can we go?" He had chosen his travelling companion well, and needed Makovitsky's devotion and unflappable temperament if he was to keep his head. Makovitsky responded by suggesting they travel south to Bessarabia to stay with Tolstoy's worker friend Gusarev, who lived with his family on his own land. "L.N. did not reply," he wrote. When they arrived at the station of Shchokina, a train to Tula was expected in twenty minutes, and one to Gorbachevo in half-an-hour. Although it was only a short distance to Shamordino from Gorbachevo, Tolstoy was afraid Sofia would wake and come after them, and wanted to travel via Tula to throw her off their tracks. But Makovitsky persuaded him he would be instantly recognised in Tula, so they took the Gorbachevo train instead.

It must be said that none of this resembles a heroic departure. Yet to this day the heart-warming image persists of Tolstoy walking off at night, with a knapsack on his back and a stick, even though there would have been nothing heart-warming about this old man of 82 "walking off", who for all his phenomenal vitality suffered from blackouts and episodes of forgetfulness, heart palpitations and varicose veins. The writer Ivan Bunin, in his book "Tolstoy's Liberation", ecstatically quoted his words in his farewell letter to his wife: "I am doing what is natural for old men of my age to do: leaving this worldly life to live out their last days in peace and solitude."

Sofia also took note of these words. After recovering from her initial shock, and after two suicide attempts, she began writing letters to him begging him to return, relying on third parties to deliver them. In her second letter, which he never received, she protested: "You write about old men leaving the world. Where have you seen that? Old peasants live out their last days on the stove, surrounded by their children and grandchildren. It's the same for everyone, rich and poor. Is it really natural for an old man in poor health to leave the love, care and attention of his family?" She was wrong. It was quite common among the peasants for old men, and even women, to wander off as vagrants, or simply to live in separate huts. They left to die, when they were no longer able to do domestic tasks or work in the fields, so as not to be a burden on the young people and an extra mouth to feed. They left when "the house was ruled by sin": drunkenness, brawls and sexual scandals. But they didn't leave their old wives in the night, with the support and encouragement of their daughters.

Let us return to the fateful night of October 27th however, and follow step by step the path of his journey.

"At 3 am L.N. woke me in his dressing-gown and slippers, holding a candle," Makovitsky wrote in his diary. "His face was distraught but resolute. 'I have decided to leave,' he said. 'You must come with me. I'm going upstairs now and you'll follow me, just don't wake Sofia Andreevna. We won't take much, just a few essentials. Sasha will follow us in a few days and bring whatever we need.'"

His "resolute" expression spoke not of composure but the resignation of a man about to jump off a cliff. The doctor noted: "Agitated. I took his pulse: 100." One wonders what "essentials" an old man in his eighties could possibly need for such a journey. But this was the last thing on his mind then; his main concern was that Sasha should hide the manuscripts of his diaries from Sofia Andreevna. He had his notebooks and fountain pen with him, and Makovitsky, Sasha and Varvara Feokritova packed his luggage and some provisions. Unfortunately there turned out to be rather a lot of "essentials", and they needed another bigger suitcase, which would be hard to collect without making a noise and waking Sofia. Between the couple's bedrooms were three doors that she kept open at night, so she would wake at the slightest sound from his room. She explained that she needed to be able to hear him in case he needed help, but the true reason was quite different: she was afraid he would escape in the night. For several months now this had been a real threat. One can even pinpoint the date when this threat hung in the air at Yasnaya Polyana, after a stormy argument with her husband on July 15th.

The following morning she wrote him this letter: "Dearest Levochka, I am writing this instead of talking to you, because after a sleepless night I find it difficult to talk. I am too anxious and may upset everyone again, and I want desperately to be calm and reasonable. I was thinking everything through all night, and it became painfully obvious to me that while you caress me with one hand, with the other you threaten me with a knife, and yesterday I felt as if this knife had stabbed my heart. The knife is the threat that you will break your promise to me and slip away if I remain as I am. So now I shall spend every night as I did last night, listening and worrying that you have left. Every time you go out and are slightly late back I shall be in agony. Just think, dearest Levochka, your threat to leave me is the same as the threat of murder."

While Sasha, Makovitksy and Varvara were packing ("like conspirators", Varvara recalled, blowing out candles and listening for any sound from Sofia), Tolstoy firmly closed the three doors leading to her room and managed to collect the suitcase without waking her. But even this turned out not to be big enough, and his overcoat and a rug had to be bundled up separately with a basket of food. Impatient for everything to be ready, he hurried out to the coach-house to wake the coachman Andrian and help him harness the horses. "Went to the stables while they finished packing," he writes in his diary. "It was so dark I lost my way and missed the path to the wing of the house, stumbled into a thicket, pricked myself, bumped into a tree, fell, lost my cap and couldn't find it, and managed with difficulty to make my way out arid return to the house. I found another cap, and headed back to the stable with a flashlight. Sasha, Dushan and Varvara arrived. I was trembling with fear that I would be discovered."(What he described twenty-four hours later as a "thicket", from which he "managed with difficulty to make his way out", was in fact his own apple orchard, which he knew like the back of his hand.)

"It took us half-an-hour to pack," Sasha wrote. "Father was flustered and kept hurrying, us up, but our hands were shaking so much we couldn't tie the straps and the cases wouldn't close. I had been waiting for this every day, every hour, but when he said 'I'm going,' it shocked me as if I was hearing it for the first time. I shall never forget him standing in the doorway of the house in his peasant shirt with a candle in his hand, and his bright, determined face." Varvara too was struck by his "bright, determined expression".

It was a bleak October dawn, and the houses in the village, masters' and peasants' alike, were in total darkness, and this old man in his peasant clothes standing at the door with a candle under his face would have startled anyone. But we shouldn't be deceived about his state of mind then. Of course his fearlessness and stamina were legendary. The pianist Alexander Goldenweiser, a friend of the Tolstoys' and a frequent visitor to Yasnaya Polyana, left a vivid description of a sledge ride in the snow with him two years earlier, to help a needy peasant family in a village four miles away: "We had reached the station of Zaseka when a snowstorm blew up. It grew fiercer, and before long we had lost the road and had no idea where we were. After stumbling around for a while we saw a forest lodge in the distance, and headed for it to ask the forester for directions. As we approached, three or four enormous dogs bounded out and surrounded the horses and the sledge, barking savagely. I confess I was terrified. But L.N. firmly handed me the reins and said 'Hold them', then climbed out, whooping loudly at the terrible dogs, and walked empty-handed past them. And in an instant they stopped barking and made way for him, submitting to him as their master. Walking calmly between them to the lodge with his flowing grey beard, he reminded me of the hero from a fairy tale rather than a frail old man of eighty."

Yet on the night of October 28th his self-possession abandoned him. His helpers left the house with the luggage and he met them with the flashlight Sasha had made him take after his ordeal in the orchard. "Our feet kept slipping in the mud, and it was so dark we could hardly see the road," she recalled. "A little blue light flickered past the wing of the house as Father came out to meet us. 'Ah, it's you,' he said. 'I managed it this time. We're already harnessing up. Let me go ahead and light your way. But why have you given Sasha the heaviest things?' he asked Varvara reproachfully, taking the basket from her so she could help me with the suitcase. He went ahead, pressing the button of the flashlight every so often to switch it off so it became even darker; he always economised; and didn't like wasting energy." Nonetheless, as he helped the coachman with the horses "his hands were shaking and he couldn't buckle the harness." Then "he sat on a suitcase in a corner of the coach-house and lapsed into despair." These sharp mood swings would follow him throughout his journey to Astapovo, where he died on the night of November 7th; his conviction that he was doing the only thing possible would alternate with apathy and painful feelings of guilt. However much he had imagined this and longed for it over the past twenty-five years, it was clear it was now in no way prepared for it, physically or mentally, and even its first stages, such as when he got lost in the orchard, presented challenges neither he nor his companions could have anticipated.

But why did his decisiveness in the house suddenly turn to despair in the coach-house?

Everything had been packed astonishingly quickly, in just two hours, the horses were almost ready, only a few minutes were left before his "freedom." Yet his spirits flagged. Quite apart from his physical exhaustion after barely sleeping, getting lost, and helping carry the luggage in the dark, there are other factors that may explain his mood then. Waking Sofia Andreevna as they packed would have resulted in a mighty row, but one within the walls of the house, known only to his inner circle. He had grown used to them, they had been a constant feature of the house recently. But already his departure was drawing more and more people in, like a snowball gathering pace with every moment that passed, and what happened soon would be the exact opposite of what he had wanted. He couldn't leave without Andrian Bolkhin the coachman, or 33-year-old Filipp Borisov, Filka, the postman and groom, who was to ride ahead of the carriage with a torch. While he was in the coach-house waiting to leave, the snowball was already growing. All the journalists, police chiefs, priests and provincial governors were still asleep, but even Tolstoy himself couldn't have foreseen how many people willingly or unwillingly would be swept up in his escape, including government ministers, the senior clergy, Prime Minister Stolypin and Tsar Nicholas II himself. Naturally he knew it was impossible for him simply to leave Yasnaya and vanish. Even Fedya Protasov in his play "The Living Corpse", who faked his suicide, was eventually caught. But he also wrote "Father Sergius", and "The Posthumous Notes of Old Fyodor Kuzmich", about famous men who retreated from the world, and it was this idea that sustained him as he prepared to cast off into the unknown, that a man's fame could exist independently of him and he could live in obscurity. It didn't matter who he had been in the past - the Russian Tsar, a famous miracle-worker, a great writer - what mattered was that here and now he could be the most simple and ordinary of men, and could dissolve into the human space, unnoticed by anyone.

As he sat on his suitcase in the coach-house in his knitted cap and peasant overcoat, it seemed his dream was finally about to be realised. Yet it was that hour, five am, "between the wolf and the dog," that anguished moment of waiting when the house was behind him and there was no going back, when the horses were almost ready and he was about to leave Yasnaya and his wife; his wife, with whom he had lived for forty-eight years, who had borne him thirteen children, seven of them still alive, who themselves had produced twenty-three grandchildren; his wife, on whose shoulders he had loaded all the responsibilities for running the estate and publishing his greatest works, parts of which she had copied out for him several times, and many other works too; his wife, who nine years earlier in the Crimea, when he was thought to be dying, had spent sleepless weeks looking after him, for only she could carry out the intimate tasks involved in his care; his wife, who might wake at any moment and discover the closed doors and disorder in his room, and find out her worst fears had been realised.

We can imagine the scene, as she burst into the coach-house and found him wrestling with the horses' harness. It wasn't so much Tolstoy as Gogol. It's revealing that Tolstoy had mixed feelings about Gogol's story "The Carriage", whose hero, the provincial aristocrat Pifagorh Pifagorovich Chertokutsky, hid from his guests in his new carriage, and was discovered in the most humiliating way. He considered the story excellently written, but a silly joke. Yet "The Carriage" isn't a joke. The arrival of the General, who discovers Chertokutsky in the coach-house cowering under the leather apron of his carriage, is the arrival of Fate itself, catching up with a man at the moment when he is least prepared for it, exposing him in all his helplessness and vulnerability. According to Sasha: "At first Father kept hurrying up the coachman, then he sat on the suitcase and said 'I'm terrified we'll be caught and all will be lost. We can't leave without a scene.'"

Tolstoy's weakness
His emotions then can be understood partly in terms of his fastidiousness and breeding. Writer, philosopher, "this colossus of a man," in Lenin's words, his temperament was that of an old-fashioned Russian aristocrat, in the finest sense of the word. This complex and alas long-lost code of behaviour involves notions of moral and physical decency, the inability to lie or speak ill of people behind their backs, the fear of hurting their feelings with a thoughtless word, and of simply being disagreeable". In his youth, his ungovernable character meant he often failed to live up to these standards, which were partly hereditary and partly instilled in him by his upbringing, and he suffered from this. But in his old age, as well as cultivating the virtues of love and compassion, he developed an even greater distaste for anything sordid, scandalous and indelicate. Throughout the whole of his conflict with Sofia he was almost entirely blameless. He pitied her, and reproached people who spoke ill of her, even when he acknowledged the justice of their criticisms. He submitted to her demands, however foolish and impossible, and patiently endured her provocations, including her attempts to blackmail him by threatening to commit suicide. But fundamentally, to the surprise and even dismay of many of his followers, at the core of his character weren't abstract principles but the nature of an old-fashioned aristocrat and a fine old man, who painfully resigned himself to his wife's insults and humiliations.

And so he secretly planned his escape, which would be more terrible than anything she could have imagined: it wasn't a knife, it was an axe. This was why his most powerful emotion in the coach-house that night was fear. Fear that she would wake, run out of the house and find him sitting on his suitcase, waiting for the carriage to be ready. There would be no way then to avoid a scene, a dreadful, heart-wrenching scene that would be the culmination of all the bitter arguments at Yasnaya recently. He had never run from his difficulties. On the contrary, he had thanked God over the years for sending him these experiences, accepting the "unpleasantnesses" with a humble heart, and rejoicing when people judged him. But now he no longer had the strength to endure them, and he longed for the cup to pass from him. Clearly his decision to leave was evidence as much of weakness as of strength, and he spoke openly of this to his old friend and confidante Maria Schmidt. A former schoolmistress, the most committed and sincere of the "Tolstoyans", who believed in Tolstoy as in a new Christ, she lived in a hut in the village of Ovsyannikovo four miles from Yasnaya. He visited her often when he was out riding, knowing that his visits didn't merely give her pleasure but were the main reason for her life, and he asked her spiritual advice on October 26th, two days before he left. When he told her of his still undecided plan, she clapped her hands.

"Lev Nikolaevich dear, it's weakness! It will pass!" she said.

Tatyana Tolstaya in her memoirs quoted this exchange between them verbatim from Maria Schmidt. However in Makovitsky's diary there is no reference to the conversation, and Maria Schmidt herself, when interviewed by "Russian Word", insisted that Tolstoy had said "not a word" to her about leaving when they met.

This was clearly not true, and is explained by her reluctance to air the family's problems in public. But on October 26th, in Tolstoy's secret "Diary For Myself Alone", he had written: "More and more burdened by this life. Maria Alexandrovna doesn't tell me to leave, but nor does she blame me." Makovitsky noted in his diary on that day that "L.N. seemed distracted and in low spirits." When riding over to Maria. Schmidt's he had done a "bad thing", he told him, and had ridden over some winter crops; it was especially bad to do this when it was muddy, and the horse had left deep tracks as it trampled on the delicate green shoots. So he cared more about the new crops than his old wife? This is how the man in the street sees him: strong Tolstoy, Lenin's colossus", leaving his weak wife because she couldn't follow him

on his spiritual path; he had to leave her because he was a genius, and it's always dangerous to marry a genius. It's a view that chimes with one popular in intellectual circles, elegantly formulated by Ivan Bunin, that he left home to die. It was an act of liberation, a spiritual titan escaping from the material prison that had confined him. There are pagan and animal metaphors of his dash from Yasnaya too, expressed in the first days of his flight by the poet Alexander Kuprin, who compared him

to some mighty beast sensing the approach of death and wandering off from the herd. But his escape wasn't that of a titan resolved on a last magnificent act, still less of an old but still powerful animal. He was a sick old man, who had dreamed of leaving for twenty-five years but hadn't done so, regarding it as cruel to his wife. And now that his family crisis had finally reached boiling point, he no longer had the strength, but saw no alternative for himself or those close to him. He left when physically he was longer capable of it, in autumn, with nothing prepared, when even the plan's most enthusiastic supporters, including Sasha, had no idea what awaited the old man in the outside world. It was precisely then, when his departure meant his almost inevitable death that he no longer felt able to stay at Yasnaya.

EVGENY VODOLAZKIN
SOLOVYOV AND LARIONOV
A NOVEL OF RESEARCH
(EXTRACT)

Translated by Arch Tait

He was born at a halt with the unexceptional name of Kilometre 715. For all its three digits, the halt was extremely small with neither a cinema, a post office, nor even a school. It consisted of six wooden huts strung along the railway track. On reaching the age of 16, he left, went to St Petersburg, entered the University, and began the study of history. In view of the surname he inherited at birth – Solovyov – this was only to be expected.

Professor Nikolsky, Solovyov's academic supervisor, called him a typical self-made man who had come to the capital with a fishcart, but this, of course, was a joke because long before Solovyov's arrival (in 1991) St Petersburg had ceased to be a capital, and there had in any case never been fish at Kilometre 715. To Solovyov's great regret as a boy it had no river or even a pond. Reading book after book about sea voyages, the future historian deplored his landlocked existence and decided to spend the rest of his days, which at that time were still a great many, on the boundary of land and sea. Along with his thirst for knowledge, it was the lure of that great expanse of water which moved him to choose St Petersburg. The remark about a fishcart would have been no more than a joke but for its hint at the overcoming of adverse circumstances so elegantly present in the expression. The historian Solovyov was in every sense a self-made man.

General Larionov (1882-1976) was quite another matter. He came into the world in St Petersburg, in a family with a long line of military officers. Every man in the family was an officer, with the exception of the future general's father who was Director of the Department of Railways. As a child Larionov had the good fortune even to see his great-grandfather (the family inclined to longevity) who was, naturally, a general – a tall, upright old man who had lost a leg back at the battle of Borodino.

Every movement his great-grandfather made, even the tapping of his peg leg on the parquet, seemed to the young Larionov to be imbued with a special dignity. Unnoticed by others, the child liked to tuck up his right leg, negotiate the hall on his left leg and, clasping the back of the divan in the manner of old General Larionov, fall back against it with a deep sigh. Larionov's grandfather and his luxuriantly moustached uncles were, in all truth, no less impressive than his great-grandfather, but neither their dashing military bearing nor their ability to express themselves eloquently (the great-grandfather was taciturn) could rival that missing leg.

The only thing which did impress the child about his bipedal relatives was their abundance of medals. His favourite was a medal awarded to one *For Quelling the Polish Revolt*. The child, who knew absolutely nothing about Poles, was enchanted by the very melodiousness of the words. Seeing how drawn he was to the medal, his uncle finally gave it to him and he would wear it, along with another, *For the Taking of Shipka*, which he received from another uncle, right up until he was seven. The word 'Shipka' was no match for the sonorousness of 'Polish Revolt', but the beauty of the medal itself compensated for its phonetic shortcoming. The child knew no happier moments than when he sat among his military relatives wearing those two medals on his chest.

These were Russian officers of the old school who knew how to use cutlery (even the nowadays all but forgotten fish knife), who debonairly kissed ladies' hands, and were the masters of all manner of niceties beyond the ken of officers of a later era. General Larionov had no adverse circumstances to overcome. Quite the contrary: he had only to absorb, to imbibe to the full the qualities of his environment, and that is exactly what he did.

The general in him began to show from early childhood when, having barely learned to walk, he lined up his wooden Hussars in orderly ranks. Seeing him thus engaged, those present uttered the only words possible: General Larionov. Hear how naturally the words combine. They are made for each other, pronounced without hesitancy and, flowing into each other, comprise a unity as integral as a horse and rider in battle: General Larionov. That was his first and only name at home, and he took to it immediately and forever. General Larionov. Hearing himself so addressed, the child would stand up and silently salute. He learned to speak only when he was three and a half years old.

What, we may wonder, coupled two such dissimilar individuals as Solovyov, a historian, and General Larionov, if, of course, one may talk of the coupling of a young, flourishing academic with a military commander worn out by battles and, moreover, already dead? The the answer is straightforward: the historian Solovyov was researching the career of General Larionov. Having graduated from St Petersburg University, he became a postgraduate student at the Institute of Russian History, and it was here that he adopted General Larionov as the topic of his dissertation. There can be no doubt that by 1996, the year in question, General Larionov did already wholly belong to Russian history.[1]

Needless to say, Solovyov was not the first to take an interest in researching the renowned general's biography. At different times a couple of dozen scholarly articles devoted to his life had been published, and these considered the still unexplained mysteries associated with its various periods. This number of papers, although at first sight considerable, appears entirely inadequate in the light of the interest General Larionov has always aroused, both in Russia and abroad. It is surely significant that the quantity of academic articles is considerably less than the number of novels, films, plays etc in which the general features either as one of the characters or as the prototype of the hero. The situation seems to symbolise the predominance of mythology over positive knowledge in all matters relating to the late general.

Moreover, as was demonstrated in a survey article by Professor Amélie Dupont, a French academic, mythology seeped even into scholarly articles about the military leader. For anyone venturing to approach the subject, then, the field of their research was truly something of a minefield. Even those articles, as Dupont also points out, in which truth is backed up by the full panoply of scholarly argumentation, throw light only on problems and episodes so particular that the significance of the truth established tends to zero. It is worthy of note that to this day Dupont's work (which has been published both in French and in Russian) remains the only monograph devoted to General Larionov.[2] This draws attention to the paucity of relevant sources. If the French scholar succeeded in garnering the material for a monograph, this was purely as the result of her dedication and exceptional attitude towards the topic, which she referred to as the main interest in her life.

Professor Dupont was, without exaggeration, created to research this Russian military commander. We are not here referring to the French historian's external appearance, which has been the object of considerable unseemly mirth within the scholarly community.[3] It is after all well known that jibes and jokes behind the back of a major scholar (Dupont is referred to as "Mon Général" in narrow circles) are usually no more than a manifestation of envy. Accordingly, in referring to Amélie Dupont as preordained to research this topic, we have in mind primarily a rare tenacity without which, in all truth, she would never have succeeded in unearthing the key sources which she subsequently published. Indeed, there may be more than a grain of truth in the surmise that the appearance of the moustache, which provoked such an infantile reaction in scholarly circles, was occasioned by the lady's single-minded pursuit of her topic. In the interests of objectivity it should be noted that General Larionov did not, in fact, have a moustache.

In all the extant photographs (see the plates in Dupont's monograph) we encounter a meticulously clean-shaven man with cropped and neatly parted hair. The parting is so straight and the shaving so impeccable that, when looking closely at the photographs, one seems to scent eau de toilette. In this, as in most other instances, General Larionov took the only correct decision. Unlike his fellow officers, he made no attempt to style himself on Alexander III, considering that his ideally symmetrical features had no need of a frame of facial hair. It is worth commenting that, for all its symmetry, his face was not handsome, although in the years of his maturity, and more particularly in old age, it appeared to become enlivened. It not infrequently occurs that, examining the photographs of a person in their youth, one is struck by a glaring infantility, the almost embryo-like nature of their appearance

1. See Who's *Who in Russian History*, Moscow, 2005, pp. 1082–8.

2. Amélie Dupont, *The Riddle of a Russian General*, St Petersburg, 1991.

3. This relates in part to the scholar's height (1 metre 87 cm) and to the fact that in her forties she sprouted a moustache.

by comparison with what came later. In such instances one regret that the person portrayed even existed at this phase in their life. Needless to say, any such reaction is highly ahistorical. As regards the general, the wrinkles under his eyes and the hook which appeared with age in his nose render his face more expressive. At a particular period in his life, in his late 30s, this hook and the expression on his face (but not his features as a whole) lent him a resemblance to Cardinal Richelieu. It was the period when the general's achievements, and the mysteries associated with them, were at their peak. His similarity to Richelieu may have been a resemblance between two men with a secret. Be that as it may, with time it too disappeared.

Even a cursory glance through Professor Dupont's illustrations makes clear that there is an unmistakable preponderance of photographs from the final period of General Larionov's life. The old man never posed for the camera but neither did he shrink from it: he regarded it with complete indifference. This attitude gave the general's portraits a naturalness unusual in the genre, which may be the principal explanation of why on two occasions they won international competitions.

Even people wholly unacquainted with the general's career or who have never heard of him will doubtless recall the black-and-white photograph of an old man sitting in a deck chair on the very edge of the quayside (Yalta, 1964). It is one of the classics of international photography, like the locomotive which has crashed through the window of a Paris terminus, or the lighthouse standing in the midst of a raging sea. Despite the heat of the summer day, the old man is sitting in a white military jacket. He is reclining beneath a semi-transparent sunshade with his legs crossed. The toe of one light-coloured shoe points forward, parallel to the ground and almost merging with the quayside, so that a lighthouse in the middle distance seems to be balanced on the toe of his stylish footwear. The old man is looking into the distance, his gaze filled with the attentiveness of someone with no interest in anything nearer than the line of the horizon. That old man is General Larionov, and it can only

be said that next to this photograph all earlier photos fade into insignificance and seem almost unworthy of so outstanding a figure. The fact that this image of him in the fullness of his maturity is the one lodged in posterity's memory must be accounted very much to the general's advantage. Perhaps his only stroke of greater good fortune was the fact that he was not shot at the end of the Civil War, something which has always been found inexplicable.

But to the point: this precisely is the riddle that historian Solovyov decided to focus his attention on. We may anticipate doubts as to whether historian Solovyov is the right person to set about disentangling so entangled a history, and whether indeed it is not folly to place reliance on someone who only recently was a student, as well as a self-made man. These objections to not appear well founded. It will suffice to point out something also first established by Dupont,[4] that Arkady Gaidar was commanding a regiment when he was sixteen and a half years old. As regards the expression 'a self-made man', the term is nowadays generally considered applicable to anybody who has succeeded in achieving anything in life.

As regards Solovyov's work on himself, let us mention just one detail: he managed to replace his South Russian accent with that of an aristocratic Petersburger. Needless to say, there is nothing discreditable in the South Russian accent as such, or anything that would detract from the dignity of those who speak with it (in just the same way as, let us say, the limping patois of Moscow has no call to discredit the citizens of our capital). Indeed, Mikhail Gorbachev undertook the perestroika of Russia with a wholly South Russian accent. Gorbachev, of course, was not a historian: he made history himself, without concerning himself unduly about the orthoepic aspect of the matter.[5]

As regards Solovyov, as he whispered Russian tongue twisters in the hostel kitchen he was engaged, in his own mind, in something greater than merely correcting his pronunciation: he was overcoming his provincialism.

An important part in Solovyov's development was played by his academic supervisor, the

4. It is, however, worth noting that the French scholar's discovery was made by chance and is associated with the main object of her research: at the end of the Civil War, when A.P. Gaidar began publishing his stories, General Larionov on more than one occasion publicly voiced his regret at not having put him up against a wall when he had the chance.

famed Professor Nikolsky. Having read his student's first essay, which was about Russia's assimilation of the Far East of the country, the professor invited him to his study and, without saying anything, took a long drag on the cardboard filter of a White Sea Canal cigarette (he had become addicted to Russian cigarettes while constructing the eponymous canal).

"My friend," the professor said when he had lit up, "scholarship is boring. If you don't get used to that, you will encounter difficulties in getting to grips with it." Nikolsky asked Solovyov to delete from his essay the words 'great', 'victorious', and 'the only possible'. He asked his student whether he was familiar with the theory that Russians squandered such energy as they had been endowed with by attempting to master impossibly extensive territories. The student was not yet acquainted with this theory and, until he was, Professor Nikolsky asked him to delete also the phrase 'progressive phenomenon'. The attention of the essay writer was particularly drawn to the formatting of bibliographical and explanatory footnotes. Close attention to this aspect of his essay indicated that the only correctly formatted footnote was one reading "Ibid., p. 12". To be completely frank, most of Professor Nikolsky's remarks struck Solovyov as nitpicking, yet it was this discussion which laid the foundation for a friendship between the professor and his student. The professor was of an age when his remarks could no longer be taken amiss by the younger man, and Solovyov's own less than straightforward history caused his supervisor in turn to be lenient with his pupil.

Professor Nikolsky never tired of repeating to his ward that fine phrases in scholarship were as a rule false, and that their fineness was premised on their supposed universality and the absence of exceptions. But, the cigarette in the Professor's hand described a smoky ellipse, that absence was illusory. There were no comprehensive truths (almost none, the professor corrected himself, bringing his maxim into accord with his own theory). For every A there will always be a B, and C, and something which cannot quite be conveyed by any letter. An honest researcher will bear this in mind, and his statements will be no

less fine for it. Thus said Professor Nikolsky.

Solovyov's blue-eyed romanticism at some point in time was replaced by a pronounced tendency to exactitude, and this was the time when he discovered a particular kind of beauty, the beauty of solidly grounded knowledge. It was a time when the young man's papers sprouted an immense quantity of exhaustive and irreproachably formatted footnotes.[6]

He added footnote after footnote and wondered how he had been able to do without them at the beginning of his academic career. When a footnote began to accompany almost every word he uttered, Professor Nikolsky was obliged to stop him and inform him casually that by the end of their careers scholars usually dispense with footnotes. The young researcher was disconcerted.

The Pacific Ocean, towards which Solovyov had been drawn in his first essay, did not, despite his expectations, become his principal topic. Professor Nikolsky succeeded in persuading his student that the most important part of history takes place on continents. Only a sound knowledge of that history conferred the right occasionally to cast off from the land. The outcome of an agonising inner struggle was that Solovyov decided to postpone taking to the seas.

In the course of his five years at University Solovyov became a real Petersburger. He began wearing good quality but unshowy clothes (as one moves towards the South, and this is true not only of Russia, clothing generally becomes more garish), referred curtly to the state authorities as "they", and became an enthusiast for evening strolls through Vasilievsky Island. Subsequently, when he rented a room in Petrograd District (11 Zhdanov Embankment), he retained his penchant for strolling. When he finished working in the library he would walk home. Garden Street. The Summer Gardens. Trinity Bridge. In the winter when, in accordance with their name, the Summer Gardens were closed and the statues boarded up, Solovyov chose a different route. By Griboyedov Canal he would walk down to the River Neva, then past the Winter Palace (open, unlike the

5. Even in his subsequent retirement, when he had every opportunity to undertake self-improvement, the statesman declined to renounce either his fricative 'g's or his voiced consonants at the end of words.

6. Footnotes became for him not merely an opportunity to express respect for his predecessors. They revealed to him that there was no area of knowledge where he, Solovyov, was a pioneer and that scholarship is a process which is hugely ongoing. Footnotes were representatives of great, all-encompassing knowledge. They followed Solovyov and fostered him, obliging him to

Summer Gardens, all year round), and turn on to Palace Bridge. Back home he would put his sodden shoes on the radiator. Salt spread by the yardkeepers turned them white by morning. Solovyov came to love the special winter cosiness of the Public Library, the figure of Catherine the Great glimpsed through a half-frosted window, the pre-war lamps on the tables, and the barely audible whispering of those sitting behind him. He liked the indescribable aroma of the library. It combined the smell of books, bookcases, and worn carpet runners. All libraries smell the same. It was the smell of the single-storey village library, half-buried in snow, from which the young Solovyov had taken out books. The library was one and a half hours' walk from Kilometre 715 station. He would go there after school before walking back to the station and home. He sat side on to the desk of the elderly librarian, Nadezhda Nikiforovna, while she looked out books for him somewhere behind the bookshelves. As he waited for her to return he would examine his indelibly purple fingers sunk in the rabbit fur of his hat. From time to time her head would appear from behind the shelves.

"*Captain Blood: His Odyssey*?"

"Read it."

He had read everything. The village library was the first amazing shock in his life, and Nadezhda Nikiforovna was his first love. Unlike the houses beside the railway track, it was very quiet in the library and didn't smell of railway sleepers. To the fairytale library infusion of smells was added the fragrance of Red Moscow perfume. This was Nadezhda Nikiforovna's perfume. If there was one thing missing from Solovyov's subsequent life in St Petersburg it was Red Moscow.

"*The Children of Captain Grant*?"

Her quiet voice made goose-pimples run slowly down Solovyov's back. Moistening a finger, Nadezhda Nikiforovna's extracted a form from the drawer and made the requisite entry. Solovyov watched bewitched the movements of her fingers with their large, dull nails. She had a signet ring with a stone on her ring finger. Reshelving books, Nadezhda Nikiforovna would snag the wood with her ring and the cameo would emit a flat, plastic sound. So different

from the rasping of the railway carriages, in Solovyov's ears the sound assumed an amazingly refined, almost aristocratic quality. He later described it as the first timid knocking of world culture at the door of his heart. Most often Solovyov did not come to the library on his own. He was accompanied by a girl called Liza who lived in the house next door. Liza was not allowed to walk home alone and was instructed to wait for Solovyov in the library. She sat some distance away, silently observing the issuance of books. Sometimes she would take something Solovyov had read. As soon as he got home Solovyov forgot all about Liza. He remembered every detail of his visit to the library, and surrendered to dreams of married life with Nadezhda Nikiforovna. It should be emphasised that at the age of eight these dreams were entirely chaste. Being far removed from the hotbeds of civilisation (and simultaneously, in Nadezhda Nikiforovna's words, from the clinker they precipitated), Solovyov had little idea of the purpose of marriage or how it proceeded. His only link with the outside world was this village library from which not only erotic publications, but even questionable illustrations in the periodical press, were rigorously excluded. Such things were mercilessly cut out by Nadezhda Nikiforovna, who censored new arrivals in her free time. There is nothing surprising in the fact that five years later, with the awakening of their instincts, Solovyov and Liza lacked any guidance whatsoever in these matters and had quite literally to grope their way ahead. However, even when later in adolescence he engaged in sexual activity, Solovyov did not consider himself unfaithful to Nadezhda Nikiforovna. Indeed, the idea of marrying her, which had so warmed him as a child, even then had not lost its attraction. What changed was only his becoming aware that there were certain things he would not be requiring of Nadezhda Nikiforovna. For the present narrative, however, Liza's surname is not without interest: Larionova. The present narrative is altogether inclined to emphasise a number of similarities and coincidences, because every simile has meaning: revealing another dimension, hinting at a true perspective without which the gaze would surely come up against a brick wall. Embarking on his researches into the life and career of General Larionov, Solovyov was mindful of his earlier encounter with the surname. He saw such matters as significant. Needless to say, the young researcher could not yet explain the part the Larionovs would play in his life, but he already sensed that it would not be a minor role.

As mostly happens with predictable events, Solovyov stumbled upon his research topic by chance. Before him it had been worked on by a graduate called Kalyuzhny, a likeable young fellow if without the least enthusiasm for research, or indeed anything else. His efforts extended only to making his way to the University bar and settling there for the rest of the day. Sympathetically inclined towards the general, and indubitably curious about his destiny, the main thing puzzling him (his finger slid over the glass of his beer mug), was how the general had survived. Over the course of several years Kalyzuhny would paraphrase to anybody who sat down at his table the classic work of Professor Dupont. This endless paraphrasing evidently exhausted him completely because, in all the years of his ceaseless narration, he never wrote a single line. Summoning all his remaining strength, Graduate Kaluzhny unexpectedly did what the general in his lifetime never made up his mind to do: he emigrated. His subsequent fate is unknown.

What is known, however, is Solovyov's fate who, in the unanimous opinion of his colleagues, was just the person to replace their departed comrade. Only a few months after embarking on his postgraduate career, he read a paper at a conference. It was titled "Researching the Life and Career of General Larionov: Results and Prospects".

The results presented and the prospects outlined by Solovyov made a highly favourable impression on his academic audience. The young researcher's paper testified not only to a well organised mind, but equally to profound interest in his topic. The high point of his paper, which caused a great stir in the hall, was his correcting of certain facts in Professor Amélie Dupont's monograph, which until then had been considered unimpeachable.

Thus, it transpired that in the 34th Infantry Division of 136 Taganrog Regiment there were not 483 soldiers, as asserted by Dupont, but only 469. It was shown also that the number of soldiers in the 2nd Native Division of the Joint Cavalry Brigade had, on the contrary, been understated by the French researcher who had given 720 (whereas the correct number was 778). Professor Dupont had not only failed to fully elucidate the role in the Crimean Campaign of Colonel Y.D. Noga (1878- ?), but had also clearly exaggerated the officer's educational level: Dupont erroneously stated that Noga had graduated from the Vladimir and Kiev Corps of Cadets when in fact he had graduated only from the Vladimir (i.e., St Vladimir) Kievan Corps of Cadets. Solovyov had a number of more minor complaints about the French monograph, but at this point it may be thought sufficient to limit ourselves to those already enumerated as sufficiently characterising the quality of the young scholar's work and his unwillingness to blindly defer to the authority of his predecessor.

This was Solovyov's moment of glory. Inconspicuous behind one of the conference hall's marble pillars, no less a person than Professor Dupont was listening to his paper. All who observed her at this moment testify that the French historian's eyes misted over. One less devoted to scholarship might have been offended by all the amendments put forward by Solovyov. They might have turned nasty, possibly even shrugging their shoulders and snorting contemptuously. They might have argued, for example, that in the wider context of explaining events in the Crimea in 1920 the proposed corrections contributed relatively little. Dupont was not such a person. As Solovyov concluded with the traditional, "Thank you for your attention", she raced from behind her pillar to embrace the young scholar. This ardent academic embrace, which involved a sob of emotion, smudged mascara, and a pricking by moustache – was it not a triumph of true values, testimony to the indestructibility of the great Internationale of research?

As she stood with her running mascara at the lectern, Amélie Dupont recalled all those who over the years had dedicated themselves to study of the post-revolutionary period. She spoke with particular warmth of I.A. Ratsimor who had initiated but was never to complete a monumental *Encyclopedia of the Russian Civil War*.[7] He died at the letter 'K', Dupont reminisced, and if he could only have lived to complete one more letter, our knowledge of General Larionov would have been on a quite, quite different level. "But now," and with these words the professor again drew Solovyov close to herself, "we see his worthy successor. Now we can leave the stage reassured."

Solovyov wanted courteously to seek to dissuade the Frenchwoman, to urge her to continue her work which was of such importance to everybody, but she was having none of it. With a grand sweep of her great arm she appeared to pluck a copy of her monograph from the air and forcibly pressed it to Solovyov's breast. Kissing him one final time, Amélie Dupont marched the length of the conference hall and vanished into the semi-darkness of the corridor.

She called him from Paris and wanted to know absolutely everything about the young scholar, his views on history in general, his preferences in methodology and even, entirely unexpectedly, his financial situation. Although he coped with all the other issues, Solovyov was completely unable to think of a coherent reply to her enquiry after his finances. She provided a concise summary herself: Russian scholars don't have a financial situation.

Shocked by this circumstance, Dupont set about establishing the reasons for such a dismaying state of affairs. Adopting a determinist position, this representative of French historical scholarship elaborated a long causal chain which it would be pointless to give here in full, since the events she mentioned are well known to every Russian schoolchild. We shall dwell only upon certain underlying principles she saw as typical of the chain.

The direction of Russian society was determined by a number of factors of which, in Dupont's view, the crucial ones were: an insufficient predisposition to hard work, a tendency to misappropriate the property of

other people, and an acute sense of justice. In the academic's mind the chain of causality assumed the form of what, upon mature reflection, she concluded was a vicious circle.

The situation as she saw it was far from rosy: misappropriation of the property of others inflamed the sense of justice to impossible levels, and this in turn greatly diminished society's predisposition to hard work. This, needless to say, could only further stimulate the tendency to misappropriate the property of others and this automatically led to greater inflammation of the sense of justice and even less predisposition to hard work. Within this context the professor reviewed Russia's destructive revolutions and the (in her opinion no less destructive) rule over many years of the Communists, and a whole series of other events. The combination of these factors was explosive enough ("a Molotoff Cocktail," she sighed), but was potentiated by the role of the individual. A succession of individuals had marched across the rickety stage of Russian history who had successfully inflated all the contradictions to extreme levels. These personalities are only too well known and of the list compiled by the professor we shall mention only Yegor Gaidar, and for two reasons. The first is that his government's actions were, in the academic's opinion, a happy exception. Despite its unprecedented scale, misappropriation of property for the first time appeared relatively civilised and was far less repulsive than usual. The second and perhaps main reason for mentioning Yegor Gaidar is the close interest our narrative has in mysterious threads running through different periods, events, individuals and so on. Unlike his grandfather, Yegor Gaidar was not acquainted with General Larionov and had not even commanded a regiment at the age of 16.[8]

He had not galloped over the dusty roads in July, had not drowned peasants under the ice in Khakassia but had, for all that, in his thirties headed a decidedly combative government. Employing military terminology, Dupont called the attempt to reform Russia's economy a typical cavalry charge.[9] Yegor Gaidar was the

7. I.A. Ratsimor, *Encyclopaedia of the Russian Civil War*, A-K, Paris-Nizhnii Novorod, 1991.

8. N. Gnatyuk, *Sud'ba barabanshchika (Destiny of a Drummer)*, Moscow, 2008.

9. See A. Dupont, "The Headless Horseman", in *Approaches to Russian Privatisation*, Moscow, 1999, pp. 48–71.

grandson of Arkady Gaidar and the historical and cultural significance of this fact had a great impact on the French academic's imagination. The article she published has a pronounced culturological character and surmises that had Yegor Gaidar been the grandson of Maximilian Voloshin, privatisation in Russia would have taken an entirely different course. "No comment," as a certain well-known Englishman remarked. There is no subjunctive mood in history, and ignoring this fact is a methodological weakness on the part of the French scholar. In the course of constructing her causal chain, Dupont has undoubtedly become confused about a whole range of matters. Thus, she manifestly much exaggerates the role of the personality in history, no doubt because she was herself working on the history of a general.[10]

Moreover, her stumbling block is the dialectic of the necessary and the random, which is so important for a correct evaluation of historical events. Although working with the material of Russian history she proves unable to make sense of it. At some point she seems even to have come to believe that necessity in our country is to some extent random. To put it another way, she proves unable to formulate coherently the cause of Solovyov's impoverished existence and then transfers all her boundless energy to working with the consequence. The quest for answers to Russia's accursed questions she then replaces with a quest for money to provide for the needs of the young scholar.

10. Is it any wonder that in her politics Dupont invariably adopted a resolutely Gaullist line?

DINA RUBINA
THE WHITE DOVE OF CÓRDOBA
(EXTRACT)

Translated by Daniel M. Jaffe

Part One
Chapter One

He decided to call his aunt before his departure, anyway. Typically, he was the first to make a conciliatory move. The important thing here was not to curry favor or pander, but to conduct himself as if there hadn't been a real quarrel – a mere trifle, a light tiff.

"So, tell me," he asked, "what should I bring you – *castañuelas*?"

"Go to hell!" she snapped. But her voice conveyed a certain satisfaction that he'd telephoned – that he'd called despite everything, hadn't flown off, chirring his little wings.

"A fan, then, eh, Zhuka?" he said, smiling into the receiver and picturing her patrician, hook-nosed face within a halo of blue-dyed haze. "We'll stick a beauty mark on your little cheek, and you'll step out onto the balcony of your almshouse like some *maja*, a juicy wench."

"I don't need anything from you!" she said obstinately.

"So be it." He himself was as gentle as a dove. "Oo-kaay…In that case I'll bring you a Spanish broom."

"Why a Spanish one?" she growled. And fell right into his hands.

"But what other kind does your sister fly around on over there?" he exclaimed, exulting the way children do when they make a fool of some ninny and jump around howling: "Gotcha – nya-nya-nya-nya-nya!"

She slammed down the receiver, but it was no longer a full-fledged quarrel, just a thunder shower at the beginning of May, so he could leave with a light heart, especially since a day before the tiff, he'd gone to the market and crammed Auntie's refrigerator to bursting.

* * *

All that remained was to round off the corners of one more matter, the *subject* of which he'd been arranging and working out (flourishes of details, arabesques of particulars) for three years now.

And tomorrow, finally, at the crack of dawn, against the backdrop of a turquoise stage set,

up from the sea foam (let's note: curative-spa sea foam) a *new Venus* would be born under his personal signature: the final wave of the conductor's hand, the impassioned chord of the symphony's finale.

Not hurrying, he laid out his favorite smooth suitcase of olive-colored leather, small but accommodating, like a soldier's knapsack: you jam it to bursting, *to the very*, as Uncle Sema used to say, *I can't* – then look, you can squeeze in another shoe.

Preparing for a trip, he always took great pains to think his outfit through. He lingered over the shirts, exchanged the cream-colored one for the navy, held up against it a pale blue tie from the bunch in his closet, a silk one…Yes: and cufflinks, of course. The ones Irina gave him. And the others that Margo had given him – he absolutely had to: she was observant.

Okay then. Now the *expert* was fittingly outfitted for all five days of *the Spanish project*.

For some reason the word "expert," uttered in reference to himself, made him laugh to the point of guffaws, even falling face down onto the divan, beside the open suitcase, and he laughed loudly for two minutes in sheer delight – he was always at his most infectious when guffawing alone by himself.

Continuing to laugh, he rolled to the edge of the divan, leaned over, opened the lower drawer of the wardrobe and, riffling through rumpled briefs and socks, pulled out a pistol.

It was a convenient Colt "Glock" of simple manufacture, with an automatic block firing pin and smooth recoil. What's more, with the help of a hairpin or nail, one could disassemble it in a minute.

Let's hope, dear buddy, that you'll spend the entirety of tomorrow's important meeting asleep in the suitcase.

Late in the evening, he left Jerusalem toward the Dead Sea.

He didn't like driving those loops in the dark, but the road had recently been widened and partially lit up; it was as if the camel-humped hills that had been squeezing you from both sides, forcing you into the desert funnel, now seemed to be reluctantly parting.

But at the intersection where the road turned after the filling station and followed along the sea, the illumination ended, and the ruinous darkness swollen with salt – the kind found only by the sea, *by this* sea – descended anew, slapping one in the face with the sudden headlights of oncoming cars. On the right, the black cliffs of Qumran towered sullenly; on the left stretched a smooth black salty smoothness with a sudden splash of asphalt, beyond which the Jordanian shore got all teary with distant lights.

About 40 minutes later, from the darkness below, a festive constellation of lights frothed and spilled: EinBokek with its hotels, clinics, restaurants and shops – a haven for the wealthy tourist as well as the dead-broke panhandler. And farther down the shore, a certain distance from the resort area, stood the gigantic Hotel Nirvana – alone and stretching its brightly lit white rooftops majestically into the night. In room 513, Irina was most likely already asleep.

Of all his women, she was the only one who would, if it were up to her, go to sleep and wake with the roosters, just as he would. Which turned out to be inconvenient: he didn't like sharing his dawn hours with anyone whomsoever, but safeguarded his store of resilient morning energy when, before a big day, his eyes were both sharp and fresh, and his fingertips were as sensitive as a pianist's, and his noggin was at perfect boil, and all cylinders were sparking in the billowing steam of that first cup of coffee.

For the sake of those precious dawn hours, he fairly often left Irina late at night.

Arriving at the hotel lot, he parked, got his suitcase from the trunk and, taking his time so as to drag out the final minutes of solitude, he headed to the huge propeller revolving at the main entrance.

"You sleeping?" he barked jokingly at the Ethiopian security guard. "I've brought a bomb."

The guy roused himself, hailed him with the whites of his eyes and mistrustfully stretched his white harmonica of a smile in the darkness: "Well, o-o-o-kay…"

They knew one another by sight. This hotel – bustling with people, and chaotic like the city, standing off to the side of the main resort area – was where he loved to arrange business meetings, the last and final ones: the very crowning symphonic chord which *the interested party* could reach only after having sawed through that not so inconsequential road between rocky teeth hanging above the sea, all held in place by braces and wires at the hands of some gigantic dentist.

And *it was true*: as Uncle Sema used to say – *the dog that trots about gets the bone.* (By the way, Uncle himself couldn't trot to save his life in that orthopedic boot of his.)

There it is, room 513. Quickly and soundlessly slipping into the slot that electronic key obtained from the bleary desk clerk: *you see, I don't want to wake my wife, the poor thing's suffering from a migraine and went to bed early…*

He'd never had any wife in his life whatsoever.

She wasn't suffering from any migraine whatsoever.

And he intended to wake her on the spot.

Irina was sleeping, as usual – rolled up in a blanket cocoon like white cheese in Druze pita.

Forever wrapping herself, burying herself, twisting herself sideways – hire some archeologists if you like.

Dropping suitcase and jacket to the floor, he tugged off his sweater in the doorway, kicked off – foot against foot – his running shoes, and tumbled beside her on the bed, still in his jeans – he got bogged down in the hilly bend of the zipper – and tee shirt.

Irina woke up, and they began fooling around simultaneously, trying to free themselves from the blanket, from their clothing, mumbling face to face:

"…you promised, you no-account, you promised…"

"…and I'm keeping my promise, you're practically mummified here…"

"…what kind of wild man are you, falling on me like this! Hold on…wait a minute…"

"…I'm hard already, can't you feel?"

"…hey you bum…just let me…"

"...who's not letting you...please, like that, just like that...and...li-i-i..."

...In the open balcony doorway, in sympathy with his rhythm, the lemon moon now shot upward over the railing with a shameless goggle-eyed "bravo!", now sank below, slowly and smoothly at first, then quicker and quicker – as if carried away by these, its first such rockings – now lengthening, now shortening each up-and-down pendulum swing. Then it stood stock still at a dizzying peak, balancing as if to view its heavenly neighborhood for the last time...then suddenly it broke loose and started to rush its tempo, speeding and speeding until it began to moan, snap, flinch without restraint, barely taking a gasp on its dash and – dying down, exhausted, it drooped off somewhere into the backwoods of heaven.

Afterward, Irina splashed in the shower, repeatedly switching the spray from hot to cold (then she jumped into bed – wet as a drowned man, and, come on, warm her up before she gets livid) – whereas he was trying to track with his gaze through the window those microscopic movements of that pale puffy heavenly body, his recent partner in fornication.

Finally, he got up and stepped out onto the balcony.

The gigantic hotel was submerged in benumbed slumber at the edge of the salty lake. Below, encircled by palms, like a polished grand piano lid, lay the pool where the delicate, yellow moon skipped about. Three dozen meters from the pool stretched the beach with its arthropod-like little mounds of plastic arm and lounge chairs piled for the night.

The freezing glimmerings of salt in the distance imparted to the motionless night an icy muteness, a wintry holiday feel – as if in wait for miracles and gifts.

Well, there was no waiting for gifts.

"Have you lost your mind: naked on the balcony?" spoke the lively voice from behind him. "Don't you have even the most basic sense of shame? There are people around, for goodness sake..."

Sometimes one wished not so much to shut her off as to softly lower the volume.

He closed the balcony door, drew the blinds and lit the desk lamp.

"You've put on a little weight," he pronounced pensively, lying back on the bed and examining Irina in her wide-open terry robe. "I like it. Now you look like Dina Verní."

"Wh-a-a-t?! Who's she?"

"Maillol's model. Take off that idiotic robe, uh-huh...now turn your back to me. Yes: the same proportions. A strong expressive hip line at the base of a slender back. And the shoulder connects so smoothly to the neck...Wowwee, what a model! A shame I haven't held a pencil in my hand for a hundred years."

She gave an "ahem," flopped into the deep arm chair beside the bed and reached for a packet of cigarettes. "Okay, come on, keep going...Tell me something else about myself."

"By all means! You see, when a woman puts on a few pounds, her breast becomes more becalming, more unsparing...more welcoming. And her skin color changes. The delicate layer of fat below the skin gives the body a more noble, pearl-like tint. A certain...mmm...transparent glazing develops, you see?"

He wouldn't at all have minded taking a nap before dawn if just for an hour-and-a-half or so. But Irina had begun to smoke, was wide awake and asserting herself. She looked as though about to call for a holy sacrifice again. The main thing was not even to acknowledge the attitude.

"And then, you know...," he continued, yawning and turning on his side, "that rhythmic swaying of the hip, the view from behind and above – can drive a person nuts if your hands..."

"Cordovin, you scuzzball!" Bending over, she hurled the empty cigarette packet at him. "You're nothing but an underhanded siren, Cordovin! Some kind of Casanova, some lowly tempter!"

"Nah," he muttered, irrepressibly dozing off. "I'm just...in love..."

All this was the absolute truth. He loved women. He genuinely loved women – their quick mind, earthy cleverness, strong eye for detail; he never tired of repeating that if a woman were smart, she was more dangerous than a smart man: for the usual shrewdness was supplemented by a truly primal emotional keenness, an ability to detect – from the surface, *by feel* – what can't be mastered by logic at all.

He befriended them, preferred conducting business with them, considered them more trustworthy companions and generally – better people. He frequently certified himself "a very female person." He always knew how to warm a woman up, and always found something to love in each.

* * *

He awoke, as usual, at 5:30. For many years now, some sort of zealous and implacable angel had taken to blowing reveille somewhere in the heavenly barracks, and at 5:30 on the dot – regardless of the dream he was having, regardless of the exhaustion that had lain him low two hours before – he was condemned to open his eyes… and, swearing, he'd drag himself to the shower.

But earlier today *they showed him that tin can* again. It's as if he's getting up, struggling to turn his body – *those* dreams always involve an immutable sequence of draggy movements – he's sitting on the bed straining to unstick his eyes… Then he sees *it standing there*, right on the hotel coffee table. Holy Mother of God! – that same *banged-up tin can* standing right there. No, he tells himself (everything per the damn dream scenario learned by heart so long ago) – not a tin can, you're such a swine, but a silver Sabbath wine goblet, an antique family heirloom, although – yes, somewhat dented on one side; but of course that's because it fell from a truck. And Zhuka, an orphan (war, winter, evacuation) – fearlessly climbed beneath the wheel herself and got it! And you, you louse, scum, swindler…went and sold it off to an antique dealer, brazenly, without batting an eye. And, most important, for a long time now you'd have been able to read what was engraved all around. You couldn't in those years, you didn't understand the odd flourishes, but now you'd be able to read them easily – it was Hebrew, after all, wasn't it?

But Zhu-u-ka, he groaned, as always (the scenario moves, the dream slides downhill; rather, torturously rolls uphill) – forgiveness a hundred times…I realized…searched for it! Why are we arguing again, for God's sake: it's standing right there! It's standing – massive, unpolished forever, heavily tarnished, barely distinguishable from a toy boat – on its silver domed base.

And he stretches out his lead-weighted hand, struggling as if through water, overcoming the thickness of dream. Stretches his hand, reaches… enough, finally, the heavy goblet, rotates it in his fingers, lifts it to his eyes. And a three-masted galleon sails upon three waves, and curling around the silver domed base, the angular – and now totally understandable letters: "**The train to Munich departs from the second platform at 10:30.**"

And only then did he wake up. Sort of wake up. Good Lord, for how long…*Forgive me, Zhuka*!

He stood for a long time under the burning hot lashes of water, then sharply turned it cold and for a minute, sighing in pleasure, scrubbed himself with the wiry loofah he brought with him everywhere.

Then he shaved without hurrying, whistling softly so as not to awaken the boa constrictor there on the bed any earlier than necessary…The splendid, plump boa, whose elastic rings pulsated ever so sweetly, could squeeze…yes indeedy. Still, he shouldn't let her get any plumper.

Painstakingly shaving his stuck-out chin (this was his main torture during every morning's shave – craggy as a hard apple, that chin with its tough-to-reach hollow just under his lower lip), he examined himself attentively in the spacious bathroom mirror.

So you've dried up a bit, guy…Uncle Sema would say: *Got all wiry*. He'd been a rather brawny kid in his youth. Often taken for a boxer even. He'd thinned down as he grew, as befitted his face. His nose had somehow…gotten bonier or something… Aristocratic sir? –your mother!

Only the crew-cut of his thick black hair (a persistent family pigment, he'd casually reply to compliments), and those just as jet-black brows, straight and nearly joined over his deep-set grey eyes, had stayed the same as before. *And then too* those vertical hyphens at the corners of his mouth always lending his face the expression of childlike friendliness, an external preparedness to stretch his lips in smile: *I love you, my big wonderful world*….Yes, that's our trump card. Maybe that's your only trump card, eh, guy?

When he stepped on tiptoe from the bathroom so as to get suit and shirt from the suitcase, it became clear that Irina was also awake – damn, what a nuisance that early bird nature of hers! – and lying in her cocoon, disheveled, in a foul mood and full fighting form. "You're running off like a coward," she said, observing him dress with a careful and mocking look.

"Ahah!" he gave her a broad smile. "I'm a terrible coward! I'm completely afraid of you and most humbly seek your good graces. Take a look at these cuff-links. Recognize them? I adore them and show them off to everyone: 'a gift from my favorite lady.'"

"From your favorite lady. You've got about a hundred of them in every city, right?"

"A hundred?! Why the heck so many? God! 'Who needs it, and who could bear it?' as my Uncle Sema from Vinnitsa used to say."

"You're such a shit, Cordovin. We decided, didn't we, that from now on we'd travel together."

She was wasting her breath. The vile communal joinder – "we" – …*The perpetually wearisome, weakening, weepy weeniness of love*… Not a good symptom. Must he really reconfigure her from lover into girlfriend? A shame, it was so good with Irina, after all. In point of fact, these last three years with her had been ideal, without any kind of base "we"… "us"… *My child, what helps us develop and thrive* is precisely our solitary keenness, that wolfish leanness, the quivering of our nostrils in premonition of a scented trail. What kind of "we" is there in that?

"Don't force me to drop my trousers again, ma-a-adam," he drawled in a silly mournful way. "My ba-a-ackside will get cold. See, my sword belt is already cinched."

All the same, he went to the bed, lay down – right in his suit – beside her, sleepy and wretched; he grabbed and ruthlessly yanked her naked hand out of the pillowcase, began to kiss it, moving up from fingers to shoulder: meticulously, skillfully, one inch at a time, murmuring something playfully doctorish.

His rule was: no affectionate diminutives. Each only by her complete beautiful resonant name. The female name was holy, to shorten it was heresy, akin to blasphemy.

And she softened up, gave a laugh from his tickling, pressed her bare shoulder toward his ear.

"You smell delicious: jasmine…green tea… What kind of cologne is it?"

"L'Occitane. They were palming it off at Duty-Free in Boston. The salesgirl there was trying so hard, she got on my conscience. 'An old established firm, an old established firm… Perfume bottles made by hand.' I bought one so she'd stop."

He sat up in bed, gave a cursory glance at his watch. "Listen, my joy, seriously: cheer up. I mean, what fun would it be to hang around a university conference with the depressing title, '*El Greco: un hombre que no se traicionó a símismo*'?"

"What does that mean?"

"What's the difference? It means, 'El Greco: a man who didn't betray himself.' A senseless theme, another senseless conference. Toledo's altogether a gloomy city, especially in rainy April… Honest to God it's better to be catching a tan here. And you can slip into one of those bubble baths, to boot…algae baths, are they? 'Madame is on holiday, Madame has the right.'"

It was one of those favorite little phrases of theirs that had been piling up over the course of three years: a remark by a salesman at an expensive store in Sorrento where Irina tried not to let herself "drop an awful wad of cash."

She gave a laugh and said, "Okay, beat it. When's your plane?"

At this point he glanced at his watch openly and anxiously. "Oooh, I've got to run! Or else I won't make it."

He jumped up, grabbed his jacket, the suitcase, turned at the doorway – blew a kiss toward the bed. But Irina had already wrapped herself up again; only the disheveled top of her head stuck out from beneath the blanket. *My poor baby, abandoned.* He set the door quietly ajar behind him.

After going down a flight of stairs, he stopped, cocked an ear to the silence of the still sleeping hotel: somewhere below, by the pool, maids were placidly exchanging echoing remarks, were dragging knotted rings of rubber hoses heavily along wet concrete.

Leaning his back against a door, he opened the suitcase zipper and took out two things: a blue knit glove for his right hand – strange, with slits at the fingertips – and his Glock automatic, sinless to date.

But then, why suddenly…so tense? He slipped the pistol into his jacket pocket, pulled off the glove, shaking his fingers like a pianist before his first bravura passage, then got his cell phone and dialed a number.

"Vladimir Igorevich? I didn't wake you?"

In answer, a grateful wave of a roar: "Zakhar Mironovich, dear fellow! Hello hello! How marvelous of you not to let me down! I've been on my feet since six and fretting the whole while. So, when's convenient for you? I'm in room 402."

"Terrific then," he replied. "I'll drop by in just a minute."

And again the pistol dove through the toothy slit of the suitcase zipper: that anxious deferential gratitude he heard in the client's voice was difficult to feign. And, after all, his ear and eye for nuance and intonation were extremely sharp, animal-like.

And it was true: Vladimir Igorevich was waiting for him, with trembling belly, in the open doorway of his suite. Interesting, those inviolable little crannies he must fight his daily morning razor through among all those warts. Why not just let the beard grow – or perhaps in the surreptitious code of these new Croesuses, a beard, like concealment, is a sign of hidden intentions?

"Bad luck," the fatso exclaimed, "to shake hands over a threshold!" He stepped aside, prepared, his right hand filled with a spatula.

According to certain roundabout information, this newly fledged collector owned some sort of factories in Chelyabinsk. Or mines? Or not in Chelyabinsk, but in Chukotka? God only knew, but it didn't matter. May Archangel Gabriel bless all who invest money in a strip of canvas smeared with casein primer and covered in oil paints.

He'd truly been waiting and obsessing: through the open bedroom doorway – a bed made up with the fastidiousness of a soldier.

The painting, a canvas stretched over a frame, was awaiting its appointed time with face turned to the back of the sofa.

How nevertheless touching these art lover-collectors were. They all trembled before that first moment when the painting was to be pierced by the x-ray eyes of an expert. Sometimes they'd even cover the sofa or arm chair where the painting was positioned with a white sheet as if to protect the *connoisseur's* precious view from any importunate colorful surroundings. The operating room's antiseptic color scheme or the child's game *of close your eyes tighter, and don't open them until I say*!

In that case, dear Vladimir Igorevich, you'll now hear a small lecture about the insignificance and ephemeral nature of this same *connoisseurship*.

He set his suitcase on the floor, tossed his jacket on top of it. "It's not a problem if I hold out my left?" he asked, awkwardly shaking (he should turn around and hold the hand out from behind his back) the collector's puffy paw, and flashing one of his most open smiles. "Arthritis for many years now, please forgive me. I sometimes cry out in pain like an old woman."

"No! Really?" the fatso said, all upset. "Have you tried 'Gold Mustache' balm? My wife sings its praises."

"What haven't I tried, but let's not go into that. You arrived just yesterday?"

"Of course! As soon as you said you'll be flying off today, and this would be the only chance to catch you, I quickly reserved a room, and like that tenor in the opera – 'at first light – at your feet.'"

Where the heck did he hear that opera, interesting. Maybe in his Chelyabinsk? No sweetheart, God forbid you lie at my feet.

A bottle of Courvoisier and two cognac snifters stood on the coffee table, but it was apparent the poor guy was worn out: he offered neither a seat nor a drink. This really is passion, I understand.

"All right then, let's get to it," said Cordovin. "I don't have much time at all."

"Just a single word," muttered Vladimir Igorevich, rubbing his hands as if screwing one into the other. "It's crucial…You, Zakhar Mironovich, must run into a broad range of people – these days even a herd of cattle knows where to invest money. And I can imagine your aversion to an acquaintanceship based on duty like ours. Don't object, I know it! But, you see, Zakhar Mironovich…as a collector, actually my age is infantile – I never had the opportunity to collect art before. Where would a run-of-the-mill Soviet engineer-inventor get the money? However, I am an experienced art lover, from my youth. I remember how it was: you show up in Moscow for a three-day business trip, suitcase at the hotel – and you're off at a trot to the Pushkin Museum, the Tretyakov Gallery…It's awkward to admit, I monkey around with paint…And, well, I read a lot of things. Your book, *The Fate of Russian Art Abroad* – I searched it out on the Internet, read it. I'd be happy to invite you to my place."

"To Chelyabinsk?" the expert asked out of curiosity. With attentive pleasure, he observed the sincere client was trying to dissociate himself from *the herd*.

"But why to Chelyabinsk," laughed Vladimir Igorevich. "I prefer to keep my collection here – at my place in Caesarea. And if today…if Cordovin himself gives a positive opinion of authorship…In a word, if you now pronounce your 'yes,' it'll be my third Falk. And the finest!"

He jumped to the sofa – despite his bulkiness, the fatso didn't lack a certain alpine gracefulness – and turned the painting face-front. He stood beside it as if on guard: tense, with a reddening bald spot, and alternating his searching-beseeching glance from canvas to expert. Had he forgotten to take his blood pressure medicine today – that was the question.

Sinking into the arm chair, Cordovin unhurriedly drew glasses from his jacket breast pocket, silently put them on and began to examine the canvas – from a distance.

The painting was a landscape. In the foreground – a shrub, behind it could be seen a dacha's fence and a small patch of path along which walked a woman, dim in the twilight. In the background – the red roof of a house and a copse of trees.

"From the Khotkovo series?" Cordovin finally muttered.

"Exactly!" Vladimir Igorevich said, lighting up. "This is what it means to be a specialist! It's actually called, *Overcast Day. Khotkovo*. Even the old lady owner remembers that precise title. Imagine: she forgot the painter's name, but the title, she says, all these years, like verses, she's remembered!"

"It happens." He sighed. "And what sort of *provenance* is there?"

"In my opinion, it's all irreproachable," the collector replied, revealing a pleasant knowledge of terminology of *the subject*. "There's a written confirmation by the owner. The old lady's the widow of an Israeli lawyer of average means, his second wife, at that. She remembers the painting on the wall the entire 25 years of their marriage; she says her husband brought it from Moscow in '56."

"Purchased? A gift? Details?"

"Nothing, unfortunately. The poor old thing has full-fledged Alzheimer's." He waved his hand. "But I think that's even better: at least it all looks like normal family circumstance. And what's really meaningful is that we're a decent distance from the Russian market with its out-and-out fakes."

That was true. As for the Russian market – you're right on point, most respected fellow. But old widows – of what particular value are they? Weak eyesight and full-fledged Alzheimer's: they don't remember a damn thing except what happened this morning.

(Before his eyes momentarily arose the entire, final, drawn out bonanza meeting when the old woman, having stroked fingers through the *packet of greens* he'd given, finally deigned to write out the paper: "Well, I forgot the title again…Take a look, Zakharik, maybe it's written on the back?" And he turned the canvas around and dictated distinctly, straining to see the non-existent inscription: *Overcast Day period Khotkovo*.)

"Shall I hand you the picture?" Vladimir Igorevich was concentrating with his entire being – to clutch and hand it over, to hold it up, to lay it out and shine a light on it…He felt the urge to circle the painting and caress it with hands and glances – completely natural, akin to being in love, a genuine collector's state of being that spreads to the respected expert, as well. Incidentally, the history of *the subject* is known even to include a grateful kissing of hands or two.

"Hold on." Cordovin removed his glasses and carefully folded the sides of the expensive fashionable frames – like the arms of a deceased. He lingered…" First of all, here's something I'd like to clarify: upon completion, do you, Vladimir Igorevich, need just my honest opinion or my actual signature?"

The fatso sighed "ah," blushed. What did you expect…An emotional person and, it seemed, a sincere art lover, not some miser who stole a factory for a song… or a mine, for that matter.

"Zakhar Mironovich! Who the heck would want his collection *ruined by a fake*!"

"Don't tell me," the other said with a laugh. "About eight years ago, I had to be the expert for a buyer. Two paintings, I remember, were being offered: by Mashkov and, by the way, Falk. Even a god-foresaken blind man with ripe cataracts in both eyes would have made the determination that both paintings had been executed by one and the same hand. Without taking a coffee break, at that. The circumstances seemed clear. However, the 'collector' lied through his teeth and in a frenzy demanded to bargain. I was in an idiotic situation. Of course in such circumstances an x-ray comparison would have been ideal – after all, as a rule, counterfeiters imitate only the visible aspect, the texture of the final brush strokes; their little hands don't achieve a coherent composition. But an x-ray assumes that both radiologist and apparatus are available."

"So then what?" asked Vladimir Igorevich with the same facial expression one has when watching the final chase in a movie thriller.

"I just got in my car without a word and left – inasmuch as I will never authenticate a forgery. But about two years later, those two cowboy twins were being exhibited at a respected auction, with a more obliging authentication by an expert from Art-Modus, and sold quite well. Quite well, indeed. For five times the price, I recall…Yes. And in the home of the legendary "Exodus" captain – the very one, the very one – I saw an enormous Malevich: two-by-three meters, a size the artist had never created. But the glorious captain had

taken an extraordinary fancy to it. Despite the frank reviews of many experts.

"You understand…Vladimir Igorevich," he continued pensively. "We're going to look truth in the eye. In recent years the hunt for genuinely valuable works of art has become increasingly merciless. An expert's authority has acquired a certain disproportionate, unjustified weight. And although this is my profession – you will, please, permit me to be open with you? – I'm loathe now to appear in your eyes a magician or wizard. I'm not a wizard."

"Good Lord, on my word!" the other clasped his hands. "I understand and completely realize, that – "

" – Now then, if you like, let's look at it a bit more closely."

Vladimir Igorevich rushed over, and carefully, with outstretched arms, handed the painting to the expert.

He silently turned it around, started examining the back of the frame and canvas… For several minutes, the silence was broken solely by the fatso's anxious nasal wheezing, bent as he was in a strained half-bow, and by childlike wails continually breaking out from the floor below, accompanied by wet smacks, and a woman's voice languorously singing out: "And I say you'll take it in the a-ass…"

"You know, of course," Cordovin finally stated, "that a serious expert evaluation is a complex matter; that is to say, besides an art critic's opinion, an array of technological analyses is essential: an x-ray, a chemical test…One can also practice sorcery through a microscope, mutter a few things about pigments, binders…Such evaluations can be obtained at an established organization of experts."

"Zakhar Mironovich!" beseeched the collector. "To hell with them, those organizations. I need your opinion exclusively. Just you yourself, what do you think?"

"No, wait. I, of course, am pressed for time, but I value my reputation more than my time. And now I wish to be as open as possible with you. You're looking upon me like on the Lord God, Vladimir Igorevich, but I, for goodness sake, don't allocate spots in heaven. The awful truth is that not under any circumstances can anyone take upon himself full responsibility for the conclusions of an expert analysis. You have, of course, read about the most thunderous art scandal of the twentieth century when an expert of tremendous experience, the art historian Dr. Abraham Bredus, took a forgery by van Meegeren for a work by Vermeer? And the recent scandal with a painting supposedly by Shishkin, but in reality by the Dutchman Marinus Koekkoek, which the Tretyakov let slip? And a certain Russian 'collector' for ma-a-any thousands of emerald ducats acquired "absolute bullshit" – by the way, I was enriched with this art term by a dealer with a good ten years of criminal past behind him. He decided to switch his racket to the antique trade since in that business there were higher profits and regard.

"But most tragic-comic of all is that sometimes in our business, the artist himself isn't in a position to distinguish his own work from a counterfeit. When Madame Claude Latour, the famous Parisian counterfeiter, was unmasked and brought before a court, that very Utrillo found himself in a ridiculous situation: he couldn't definitively answer whether the painting had been forged, or executed by him. And Vlaminck boasted that he'd once done a painting in the style of Cézanne, who acknowledged it as of his own creation."

"But…then what the heck?" helplessly exhaled the collector. "So where's the guarantee?"

"There can't be any guarantee, my dear!" Cordovin angrily exclaimed. "What kind of guarantee: the world's museums and private collections are cluttered with forgeries, for all their chemical analyses, x-rays, infra-red and ultraviolet lights! Do you suppose that a master-counterfeiter is dumber than us, the experts? One encounters genuine virtuosi among them, high-class professionals. They become incredibly well-versed in the methodologies of expert evaluations, learning all the technological criteria of authenticity – even the psychology of the experts themselves!"

"Then how the heck can anyone be…"

Cordovin took a handkerchief from his pocket, unhurriedly wiped his glasses and put them on – *I've raised the dead*. With evident satisfaction,

he inspected his client. Excellent work: the fellow had reached the necessary freezing point. Now we'll get down to defrosting and reanimating…

"How can anyone be?" he repeated. "By looking and seeing. I prefer to draw conclusions based on the paint layer. That's what will never let you down or deceive you – assuming you know how to read it. Everything's right there: the painting's style, emotional rhythm, individual brush strokes, the means of applying paint – everything characteristic of this, and only this, artist…The way you know in the case of a spy who's altered his appearance: the shape of brows and nose, hair color – all's been changed… but he takes a single step with his left foot, and bingo! That very left foot is what unmasks him. Although, of course, one can't deny the significance of technological expert evaluation. And it's your right to conduct one later. As for me, I simply look at the canvas and – yes, I suppose the authorship to be Falk's, and I'll now explain why: but I ask you to bear in mind that this is simply my supposition based exclusively on experience, that is to say, on intuition, and more precisely – by sniffing like a dog, forgive the vulgarity of expression."

He leaned back into the chair, his left hand balancing the landscape on his knees…

Now that the overture had been played through, that all the major themes of the symphony entitled "Birth of a New Venus from Sea Foam" had been heard, one could switch to loose variations. He loved these sudden switches to meaningless yarns, gossip about the greats, instructive stories about some passerby…It reminded him of the prelude to love when any impatient movement could crush the growing sweet languor, the craving for possession of – in our situation – a painting rather than of a woman, but it was one and the same. Venus had already come to life…One could say, the tangled red top of her head has already appeared among the foaming waves…Anyway, it wouldn't be bad to straighten the client up, otherwise – the man wasn't young after all – he might even *get lumbago*. And then, indeed, some "Golden Mustache" would be called for.

"In the eighties, in Moscow, on Lavrushinsky Lane, lived an old invalid who moved about on two crutches… So have a seat, for God's sake, Vladimir Igorevich, and relax. Sit right there, opposite; at the same time, take an extra look at your Falk. That's the way, old fellow. He participated on a commission of experts at the Pushkin Museum. Not the one on Volkhonka Street, but the other, the literary one, On Prechistenka. But that's of no importance. When the museum intended to acquire its next painting, they of course convened the commission and all the experts had their say: but the old fellow remained quiet. They let him speak last. Then everyone lapsed into silence, and he leaned over the underside of the canvas and sniffed at it. You understand? He sniffed for a long, long time…And announced his verdict. Nobody knew what he smelled there, in all those old canvases. But they trusted his hairy nostril more than any instrument. You'll agree, this all hardly resembles scientific method. What kind of science is it really – a connoisseur's sheer intuition. However, both art dealers and you collectors make little use of our suppositions. You demand uniform positive conclusions, isn't that so? Look how you worry and want – I see you want very much – for me to acknowledge Falk's authorship! Draw nearer, a little closer…"

ALEXANDRA MARININA
THE CITY RATE
(EXTRACT)

Translation by Andrew Bromfield

Hopelessly stuck in the traffic, Nastya cursed the laziness that had made her accept the offer of an official car from her new boss, Bolshakov. It would have been so much quicker by metro. Of course, if only she'd bothered to think for just a moment, she wouldn't have taken the car, but everything happened so fast, she was caught on the hop. First thing in the morning she'd made time to visit an important witness in a murder case – the killing of a banker's widow, whose husband had been murdered himself only recently. After that, she'd dropped round to the investigator's office to report, dashed across to headquarters on Petrovka in a real lather and started getting to grips with all the paperwork she'd been putting off for two weeks. And then, out of the blue, the investigator from the Municipal Public Prosecutor's Office, Fyodor Davydov, phoned to tell her Milena Pogodina's car had been found somewhere and she had to get over there. Nastya couldn't even think who Milena Pogodina was at first and when she realised, she felt really annoyed and frustrated: this was something she could have done without. Of course, Korotkov had warned her in the morning that the investigator might call, but she'd just put the idea straight out of her mind, gone ahead and planned her work for the day and then – wham! But at least the investigator was Davydov: Nastya had known old Fyodor Ivanovich for a long time and she knew there was still a thing or two she could learn from him. Before setting out for the address where the missing woman's vehicle had been found, Nastya followed procedure and phoned Bolshakov, and he suggested she should take an official car. And she did ... So it was her own fault she was sitting in this traffic jam – and that she'd have to make excuses to the investigator for turning up when the examination was almost over. Monday had started things off with a real fiasco yesterday and now the rest of the week was down the tubes.

But things didn't turn out too badly, after all. When Nastya reached the address Davydov had given her, the examination had only just begun – everybody else must have got stuck in traffic jams of their own. The car had been opened up already and the forensic technician had got to work inside it, checking the contents of the glove compartment.

"So what do we have here?" Nastya asked as soon as she'd said good morning to the investigator.

"A car, as you can see. But the address is good," Fyodor Davydov replied mysteriously.

"How's that?"

"A certain Oleg Kanunnikov lives in this building, rents a small flat here. Our missing Pogodina spoke to him on the phone quite a lot and the last time was only yesterday, about two o'clock in the afternoon. And in point of fact, he was the very last person she did speak to on her mobile. After that, there's nothing but unanswered calls. You get the general drift?"

"And what about Sedov? Where's he?"

"Where else would he be?" Davydov muttered angrily. "Hanging round my neck like a stone, thinks no one can make sense of anything here without him. He's over there, having a smoke."

Davydov pointed to a tall, strongly-built man who was hovering beside the car, shuffling his feet nervously. He kept trying to say something to the technician. Yes, that was him all right, Pavel Sedov. Nastya remembered him, though not very clearly.

"Does he know who Kanunnikov is?" she asked.

"Says he's never heard the name before."

"But does he at least have a theory?"

"His *guess* is that he's the lecturer she went to see to finish off her odds and ends of coursework. He hasn't got any other theories."

"And what's the real story? Have you identified this character?"

"Not yet, not entirely. Of course, I've sent a man to the university but the local militia officer is certain Kanunnikov's not the academic type. And his mother confirms that her son is more into construction work than jurisprudence – we got Kanunnikov's passport details and phoned the address where he's registered in Moscow. His family say he went away on a business trip for a few days. But as for the organisation that sent him, they're totally clueless on that score. Some construction firm or other, they say, but they don't have any name or address."

"And no one answers the door of the flat?" Nastya said. It was more of a statement than a question.

"That goes without saying."

"Are you going to have it opened?"

"We-ell now, what do you think?" Davydov said with a smile. "The local man will be here with a locksmith any minute – then we'll offer up a prayer and go at it. What's got you so surly? Short of sleep?"

"No, I slept all right, it's just that the day's all shot to hell."

"Well, I'm in the same boat. Can't be helped, Nastyukha, that's the way our life is. D'you reckon I was over the moon when Sedov over there and his girlfriend were suddenly landed on me? I'm up to my eyes in work already. And listen, what have you done with that Afanasiev of yours? You've got a new boy now instead."

"That's exactly what he is all right, a boy," Nastya said with a shrug of annoyance. "And brand new. Just started yesterday."

"Well, well. The young generation on the way up. And how is he? Does he know the ropes?"

"Who knows? How can you tell from just one day? Fyodor Ivanovich, does Sedov rule out the idea that Kanunnikov is his girlfriend's lover? Or does he know for sure that she doesn't have a lover? What made him think the lecturer lived here?"

"Oh-ho, so many questions, Nastyukha!" Davydov laughed in his rumbling bass. "There's been no mention of a lover so far, I don't know why. Either Pavel is absolutely certain of his live-in girlfriend, or he knows for certain that the lover is someone else. Ask him yourself, if you like."

"You mean you haven't asked?"

"Not yet. It's too soon. The man's already stressed out and it's a touchy subject. We'll open up the flat first, then tell him the bitter truth. Or he'll see it for himself – the truth, that is."

"The truth? You mean you're sure that Kanunnikov and Pogodina …"

"Oh, come on now, Nastya," Davydov interrupted, watching the movements of the technician sitting in the car. "Don't try to write me off before my time, I'm not a total halfwit, I had a good long talk with Kanunnikov's mother while I was in the car on the way here. And she told me her son and Milena Pogodina have known each other for about six years and their love is so strong, it's frightening, it's proof against any disaster that life can throw up. And the only

reason they don't get married is because they don't have a place to live, and Oleg wants to earn some money first, and buy a flat and then have a family. Makes good sense, doesn't it?"

"It does," Nastya said with a nod. "But what about Milena living with Sedov? How does that fit into the picture?"

"Well, it doesn't," the investigator admitted, "but Kanunnikov's mother doesn't know about that. She thinks Milena lives in some hostel or shares a rented room with a girlfriend. Or something of the kind, give or take."

"An interesting scenario. But …"

"Ah, here's the local man with the locksmith," Fyodor Davydov interrupted her again.

The local militiaman – a very well-proportioned, attractive thirty-something in a uniform that fitted well – held his hand out to Nastya and introduced himself.

"Captain Doroshin. Just call me Igor."

"Anastasia," she replied.

Captain Doroshin … She'd heard that name before somewhere. Or read it, maybe? There was a famous singer called Doroshin, but it was definitely a militia captain that she'd heard about. Yes, of course, in January she'd read a report on the results achieved last year by the Moscow branch of the Interior Ministry, and it had mentioned a Captain Doroshin, in the section about involving "other services" in solving crimes and tracking down criminals. What crime was it now? Murder? Yes, that was it: some businessman's wife who was murdered near the opera house. That was why Nastya remembered it, because the opera house was mentioned – a very rare event in the context of "businessmen and murders": the usual thing was country houses, restaurants, casinos and offices.

"Fyodor Ivanovich," said the technician, sticking his head out of the car, "you can take a look now. Nothing special, just the usual girly clutter."

"Aha, just a moment."

Davydov turned to Nastya:

"I'll take a quick gander in there, then we'll go up."

"Hey, boss," the locksmith called, started to get agitated, "how much longer do I have to wait?

The captain over there pulled me off an enquiry, get a move on, he said, this is urgent business, the investigator from the prosecutor's office is waiting, so I dropped everything and came running, but now I see you're in no great hurry. I've got work to do, you know."

"I'll go up with you for the time being," the captain said amicably. "We'll take a look at the door and you can choose your tools. And we have to warn the neighbours we're going to break in, or they'll get the wind up when they hear the racket and call out the duty detail from the station. And while we're at it, we can try knocking and shouting a bit. Maybe the man of the house is home, but he's asleep or up to something else and that's why he doesn't open up. Come on, let's go, the investigator's got his job to do, and we've got ours."

He gave Nastya a jolly wink that somehow made everything seemed funny. A really nice guy.

They hadn't found anything in Milena Pogodina's car that might suggest what had happened to its owner. No notes, no addresses on pieces of paper, no threatening letters. Just the usual stuff: a couple of street atlases of Moscow, a few music CDs, sunglasses, paper tissues, a powder compact, a folding umbrella, a ballpoint pen, a little notepad with nothing written on it and a few other bits and pieces.

"Hi-de-hi," said Davydov, heaving a sigh. "What a rotten, thankless job this is. You know what's going happen now, don't you, Nastyukha? We'll enter the flat and catch the lovebirds indulging their sexual appetites, so to speak. And apart from the scandal because they'll say we've violated Mr. Kanunnikov's right to personal privacy, our Pavel here will wade in, fists flying, and start having it out with his girlfriend in public. Just what we need, eh? But what option do we have? The case has been opened, and we have to search for the girl who's gone missing. But who was the jerk who opened it, eh?"

"Have they started going round the flats?" Nastya asked instead of answering.

"We've done everything we could. We managed to get quite a lot of things done while you were on the way. Of course there's no one at home now, they're all at work, but when someone did answer the door, we had a talk with them. And it helped that they sent us a whole three detectives from the district, that moved things along a bit faster. One of the occupants saw Pogodina get out of her car and walk into the entrance yesterday afternoon, about half past two."

"Is he quite certain it was Pogodina?"

"Quite sure, Nastyukha. He's seen her plenty of times, he couldn't be mistaken."

"And did anyone see Kanunnikov after that?"

"Nothing doing there. Not after that or before that. Nobody we've been able to talk to so far happened to see Kanunnikov yesterday, but that's not surprising. What is surprising is that someone noticed Pogodina and remembered her. Nobody remembers anybody else's face or takes any notice of anybody these days. No one in this house seems to know Kanunnikov, for instance, but the girl *was* noticed. She must be something special. Right then, let's get up there and take a peek at what's in this little flat."

They set off towards the entrance. Pavel Sedov, who was standing about twenty feet away, dropped his half-smoked cigarette on the pavement and followed them with a determined air.

*   *   *

Nastya had never regarded herself as a great expert on examining crime scenes. There was an investigator, and a forensic technician, two detectives from the "slaughter" division of the district criminal militia had already arrived, the district team, including a forensics analyst and a forensic pathologist, had already been called, and they'd show up any minute now, even the criminal prosecutor was going to come, so there really wasn't anything for Nastya to do in Kanunnikov's flat. Especially with the witnesses and Pavel Sedov there as well. Too many people for a small one-room flat. Milena Pogodina's body was lying in the room, and even Nastya, with her superficial knowledge, could see she'd been strangled about twenty-four hours ago.

"Igor," she said, touching the local captain on the sleeve. "Let's get out of here and have a talk."

They went out onto the landing and up one flight of steps. Nastya immediately sat down on the

windowsill and took out a cigarette, but Doroshin started fidgeting, turning his head this way and that, taking short sharp breaths in through his nose, as if he was sniffing at something.

"What is it?"

"That smell. Can't you smell it?"

"No." Nastya sniffed, but she didn't smell anything unusual. "What kind of smell is it?"

"Urine, I reckon. Don't you think so?"

"I don't know." She shrugged and inhaled. "I've been smoking for so many years, it's blunted my sense of smell. Don't you smoke?"

"No, so my sense of smell is quite keen."

He walked quickly up another flight of steps, and a few seconds later she heard his voice from up there.

"Just as I thought, someone's been relieving himself here without holding back."

"Street bums?"

"Not very likely, I move the bums on."

He came back down, squatted on his haunches beside the windowsill and started looking for something.

"There," he said triumphantly, pulling a tin can full almost to the top with cigarette butts out from behind the radiator. He held it up to Nastya's face: "See?"

"The usual staircase ashtray," Nastya responded indifferently. "You can find them in every building. "When someone isn't allowed to smoke in the flat, he goes out on the stairs, and every half-decent persecuted smoker has a can like that out there for his ash and dog ends."

"Agreed. But not many people go very far from their flat for a smoke. Only those who live on the ninth floor would smoke on this windowsill. But there isn't anyone on the ninth floor who does, I can guarantee you that."

"You know the domestic scene here that well?" Nastya enquired sceptically.

Doroshin laughed.

"It's probably the only part of my job I do know really well. Look here, there are four flats on the ninth floor. Pekarsky from number 105 rents his flat out. Kanunnikov lives there, we already know that: he's alone, and there's no one to persecute him, even if he does smoke. In 106 there's a married couple, with no children, but he's had

the wheels of his car stolen twice, so I've been in there. The air's so thick you can hardly catch your breath, and both of them smoke, husband and wife. In 107 we have a young lady with two dogs, a non-smoker. And in 108 a solitary old pensioner who recalls the days of her youth every so often and smokes a few *papiroses*. But these ..." – he lifted up the can of butts again – "... are filter cigarettes. And they were smoked by someone who came in from outside. He sat here for a very long time, smoking and waiting for something. Every now and then he went up one flight to take a piss. Does that sound right?"

Nastya nodded slowly. It did, but only if you made a lot of assumptions.

"It could have been a young couple," she objected. "No cosy corner of their own, and even if one of them happens to live in the building, they came up here to be alone together, so their parents wouldn't catch them at it, Suppose one of them smokes, and this is their regular spot, then it's not really surprising to find their permanent ash tray here. This is where they wove their little love nest. How does that sound?"

"That sounds right too," Igor agreed. "But a young lad in love isn't very likely to tell his heart's desire: 'Hang about for a moment, I'll just go and take a leak'. That doesn't sound right at all. Of course, cynicism and crudity are thriving nowadays, but not to that extent. Maybe there is a young couple lovey-doving here, but it definitely wasn't them who used the landing outside the attic door as a public toilet. Let's check something."

He took a thick A4 notepad out of his bag, tore off a clean sheet and tipped the cigarette butts out on it. Nastya noticed that right from the start he'd been holding the can very carefully, by the top and bottom rims.

"Look here," said Doroshin, stirring the butts about with a pencil and not touching them with his fingers. "The cigarettes were all the same brand. And not a cheap one, by the way. Not a single trace of lipstick anywhere, so the smoker was most likely a man. Imagine a fifteen- or sixteen-year-old kid who can afford to smoke cigarettes like this. In other words, he always has pocket money to spare, he buys his own smokes and doesn't bum them or nick them from his parents. Can you picture him?"

"Not very clearly," Nastya admitted. "I hardly ever come into contact with juveniles and I don't know that milieu very well."

"I can see that," the captain said with a smile. "But I know them very well. Believe me, a boy who always has money in his pocket and always smokes the same expensive cigarettes wouldn't hide away from his parents with his girl. He's the wrong psychological type for that. There are exceptions, but they're very rare. A boy who always has money in his pocket would take his girl to a bar."

"And where would they do their smooching?" Nastya asked with a sly smile. "In the bar?"

"These days kids like that don't smooch," Doroshin retorted very seriously. "They have sex, the whole works. But not here, in open view."

She hopped down off the windowsill, gasped and winced, snatching at her back.

"What is it?" the captain asked sympathetically. "Your leg?"

"My back. Hang on Igor, I'll just be a moment."

Nastya went down to the flat and found Davydov. The investigator didn't really seem to be listening to her, and she started feeling like an interfering fool who ought to mind her own business. But it turned out that Fyodor Ivanovich had heard everything and understood it perfectly well.

"So then either the killer is Kanunnikov himself, or the perpetrator waited for Milena Pogodina to get here, he was stalking her. Excellent! Seva! Come over here!"

The forensic technician stuck his head out of the kitchen.

"What is it, Fyodor Ivanovich?"

"Get out on the stairs and collect a tin can of cigarette ends and secretions, they'll show you where. And put that camera down, will you, you can clickety-click to your heart's content later!"

The technician put on a resentful face, grabbed his little case and walked out of the flat.

"Just a kid," Davydov sighed dejectedly when he left, "can't get enough of playing with his toys. He loves to photograph the crime scene – just has to do it, no matter what. Some

investigator or other once complimented him on his photo layouts, told him the focal shots were excellent, and his wide angles were an absolute masterpiece, so now our Seva thinks he's a top-flight photographer, and he does everything else with just a lick and a promise. And I can't say a word, he could take offence, might even resign, God forbid, and we're short of technicians already They've axed so many jobs and put in a stack of places for boffins instead, but where are we going to find that many people with the right degrees? And who's supposed to go out to the crime scene? The analyst, is it? In some districts at least they divide the jobs up, some stick to doing the analyses, and others always visit the scene, but everywhere else the boffins work on a 'first come, first served' basis. So what do we end up with? They've added the jobs, taken on the people, but there's nobody anywhere to train them right, no way they can really get the hang of anything. Today I'm Punch, tomorrow I'm Judy and the upshot of it all is, I can't learn my lines properly for either part. But a forensic technician is someone specially trained to work at the crime scene. And those are the ones they've axed. So now forensic technicians are like sacred cows, wo have to treat them very carefully, never lay a hand on them and never say a word to hurt their feelings. In some places, to keep hold of people they've moved them into Patrol and Inspection Service jobs, and those are sergeant level, so apart from the loss of prestige, their pay's gone down too, and it's no wonder they come back with: 'I'm an a Patrol and Inspection militiaman now, I don't have to do this ...' I'd love to get just a glimpse of the high-up who arranged the whole thing. I wouldn't punch him in the face, of course, just take a look him, out of curiosity. Maybe he has some special kind of pointy head, specially designed to make it harder to solve crimes. Hi-de hi, what a life ... And who found the cigarette ends? You, I suppose, sharp-eyes?"

"No, it was the captain. "Good for him, he's a fine fellow. And the spot that was used as a public convenience? Was that him too?"

"Yes."

"He's a fine fellow twice over then. I'll ring his boss and tell them to give him a bonus for helping the investigation. Oh, and by the way, the man I send to the university has called in already. Just as expected, they don't have any lecturers called Kanunnikov on the books."

"And have you told Sedov?"

"About Kanunnikov being his common-law wife's lover? No, I haven't told him yet."

"Why not?"

"There's no hurry. So I tell him, and then what? The man will fall apart. He's just barely hanging on after all he's been through already. He found his woman dead, how easy do you think that is for him? And then he gets this news on top of everything else … I'll wait for a while. Especially since Kanunnikov's mother isn't the kind of witness whose testimony you can rely on without checking. Who knows what stories her darling son might have told her? She's not even really sure where he works. They haven't lived together for five years and she doesn't know for certain what he does for a living, so we can't be certain about the connection with Pogodina. When we get finished up here, I'll send a man over to talk through the hard facts and details with her, get his whole life story clear. And I'll send a man to Pogodina's parents too. If they confirm the connection with Kanunnikov, then I'll tell Sedov. And anyway …"

Fyodor Ivanovich nudged Nastya gently towards exit of the flat. Once they were out on the stairs, he closed the door and said in a low voice:

"I don't like this Sedov. He's too bigheaded by half. Of course, he's an injured party, but I just have a feeling that we shouldn't tell him everything."

"Why?"

"I don't know. I don't trust him. I'll have the body identified first, and then we'll see."

"Identified?" Nastya was so astonished, she almost dropped her bag. "You mean you still have doubts?"

"How shall I put it? The victim's passport is in her handbag and, to judge from the photo, everything seems to be in order. Sedov himself alleges that the dead woman is his common-law wife, Milena Yurievna Pogodina, but you and I don't know that, do we? Never mind what he alleges … Fake passports are a dime a dozen

nowadays, buying one's no problem, especially if you work in the militia. Maybe it isn't Pogodina back there in the flat at all, and at this very moment Milena Yurievna is far away on some distant island, covering her tracks as previously agreed in secret with her cohabitant Sedov. Who knows what kind of shady business she might have got mixed up in! Let her parents identify her first, and then I'll be certain."

"And what if her parents are in on it too?" Nastya suggested. "Suppose Pogodina really did get involved in something criminal and she had to disappear, and Sedov warned her parents they'd have to identify a complete stranger as Milena in order to save their daughter's life?"

"It happens," Davydov said with a nod. "Everything happens. That's alright: I'll find people who can identify her, people Sedov couldn't have roped in. I'll find them all right, don't you worry about that. You know how stubborn I am, when I take a dislike to someone, hell can freeze over before I'll trust him."

Nastya knew that was the way it was, but even so Fyodor Ivanovich's theory seemed fanciful in the extreme. Milena Pogodina was a first year student in the faculty of law, so what shady business could she possibly have got mixed up in? She had no education, no profession, she hadn't even worked anywhere since she met Sedov, and before that she was a sales girl in a grocery store, and then a secretary in some small office. At least, that was the way Sedov told it. Everything could be far simpler, even assuming that Sedov was lying. He could have found out Milena was cheating, killed her and set the whole thing up to throw suspicion on Kanunnikov – end of story. And that was why he kept doggedly pretending that the idea of Milena being unfaithful had never even entered his head. But if Sedov was telling the truth, then Milena had been killed by her lover, Oleg Kanunnikov. Or if not Sedov and not Kanunnikov, then some third party, the one who had waited patiently for her, sitting on the windowsill between the ninth floor and the door of the attic.

She glanced sideways at Captain Doroshin, who had been standing by that windowsill all this time, writing something in his thick notebook. Davydov was right, he was a fine fellow, with a good head.

And cultured manners too. That was really strange. Yesterday Nastya had acquired a smart, cultured boss, and today she'd met a smart, cultured local officer. Where had the militia got all these smart, cultured people from all of a sudden? It had to be one of those amazing coincidences, the kind that happen in fairytales.

*   *   *

The two men walked slowly along the path between the graves. A cold November drizzle was falling and the older man was holding an open umbrella over his head. His companion, about ten years younger, walked along behind, bareheaded, with the water streaming off his hair onto his cheeks and neck. They stopped beside a gravestone from which the faces of a woman and a teenage boy gazed out at them. The inscription was terse – "Larisa and Georgy Bezborodov" – with the years of their lives, but no precise dates. The older man laid an armful of dark-red roses on the grave, and the younger one put down four modest carnations. They stood there for a while without speaking until the older man finally broke the silence.

"So, how are you getting on, Boris?"

"Surviving," Boris replied calmly. "Everyone survives, and so do you."

"You haven't got married again yet, to that nurse's aide of yours?"

"She's not a nurse's aide, Sasha. She's a nurse. Is it really that important for you to humiliate me?"

"All right, so she's a nurse, that's not much of a difference. She's still a village biddy with two children, no matter what you call her. So have you married her or not?"

"We've registered a marriage," Boris replied distantly.

"When?"

"Two months ago."

"So you've really gone and done it," Sasha – Alexander Kumaev – said, in a voice filled with contempt. "Not only have you betrayed Larochka's memory, you've actually made it legal. How could you?"

"Sasha, calm down, will you?"

"I won't calm down! You drove my sister to her death, you destroyed your own son's life, and now you're prepared to say to hell with it, forget it, just brush it off and marry someone else! How can I calm down? Well, well?"

Alexander had raised his voice until he was almost shouting. His pain was genuine, not affected, Boris realised that. Alexander Kamaev had loved his younger sister very much and he still mourned her loss to this very day, even after many years had passed. And although Boris Bezborodov thought what he said was unjust, he didn't try to argue because he respected his relative's grief.

"I'm sorry, Sasha, but everybody's different," was all he said.

"Yes, everybody's different. Some remember their loved ones all their life and others betray them and prefer to forget," Kamaev said angrily.

"No, Sasha. Some people prefer to weep for themselves and be miserable, while others prefer to rejoice in life. That's where the difference lies."

"That's just empty rhetoric. I weep for Lara and Georgy, not for myself

"That's not true," Boris objected firmly. "It's a lie you use to comfort yourself. In actual fact, you are weeping for yourself. We say we're grieving for the dead, but we're really grieving for ourselves, surely that's clear? We suffer without them, we're lonely, we miss them. We want to see them, touch them, talk to them. But they're not here with us and so we suffer. Do you understand what I mean? Do you hear how many times I've used the pronoun 'we'? We, us ... It's always about us, not about the ones who have died. WE suffer! And that's what makes us sad. But the person who has left us isn't suffering. If the soul is immortal, then it's in heaven and it's happy. And if there is no immortality of the soul, then there's no way the departed can be suffering. So why grieve for them? No Sasha, you're grieving for yourself. It was your personal choice, and you have a right to it. But you can't demand that I make the same choice."

"I wonder what it is that you've chosen?" Alexander laughed contemptuously. "You could have stayed in Moscow, but you went away to some dump of a village, forgot about Larisa and found yourself some semi-literate peasant woman with two children who washes your smalls, pickles cucumbers and raises chickens. Is that your choice? A man has no right to rejoice in life when his loved ones die."

"You're wrong, Sasha, if that was true, then only little children would rejoice in life, because we all start losing our loved ones early on. Great-grandmothers and great-grandfathers, grandmothers and so on and on ... The world would be filled with nothing but black, unbearable grief. But that's not the way things are, is it?"

"Don't play games with words," Kamaev said with a frown. "You know perfectly well what I mean. I'm talking about betraying the memory of the departed. When members of our family die, we can't find ourselves new ones. We don't find another mother, another father, another brother or sister. We don't betray their memory. But we can find a new wife. And a new child too. And that's nothing but betrayal, cynical and abominable betrayal. Especially if it was your fault that your wife and child died. And it was your fault that Larisa and Zhorik died, and you have no right to forgive yourself, you should suffer for it until the day you die. But look at you, you've chosen to rejoice in life! You're dancing on their graves! Aren't you ashamed of yourself?"

"No," Boris sighed, "I'm not ashamed. I do the work I love, I heal people, I save their lives, I'll bring happiness to one woman and her two children, who'll spend at least part of their childhood in a complete family. What out of all the above should I feel ashamed of?"

"You'll never understand me," Kamaev said bitterly. "We speak different languages, I always said so. I talk about one thing and you talk about something completely different. You just don't want to understand me, because you don't have any answers to give. You can stop coming here, you've no business at Larisa and Zhorik's grave. You're not worthy to be here."

"Are you serious?" Boris asked in amazement.

"Absolutely. Let's say I forbid you to come."

Bezborodov shrugged, leaned down and rearranged the flowers on the grave, then he straightened up and looked at Kamaev.

"You never cease to amaze me, Sasha. Do you really believe you can forbid me to do anything?

I live my life the way I think is right and that's what I'll keep on doing. And I'll come to the cemetery as often as I think necessary. If you don't like it, that's your problem, not mine. And if you like to spend your life grieving and mourning, that's your problem too, but it's not mine. And there's something else I have to say to you, not as a relative, but as a doctor. In your place I would think very carefully about why you made that particular choice and no other. Delve a bit deeper into yourself. If you can find the reason, you'll feel a lot better, I promise you."

Boris turned and walked slowly towards the way out. Alexander Kamaev watched him go with a glance in which contempt and hatred mingled with a completely different feeling, one of which he was only vaguely aware, although it has a very specific name: fear.

MASTER CHEN (DMITRY KOSYREV)
PET MONKEY OF THE HOUSE OF TANG
(EXTRACT)

Translated by Polly Gannon

The Book of Necromancers

The hero is caught in a fog, in the midst of a dreadful and a wondrous story, groping to find his way. He is surrounded by enigmas at every turn and can't begin to fathom the direction from which deadly arrows are flying. Lo! He hears the heavy, cruel word *war*, which cuts through the fog like an icy wind and begins to disperse it.

Chapter One
The Witch on the Roof

The dwarf advanced along the even white sand of my garden path making surprisingly rapid leaps, resembling the big red ape in the Imperial Zoo. The distorted shape of his body, wrapped tightly in dark rags and illuminated by the garden lights in the dusk, seemed to spread over the earth. From the rags protruded bare legs, set unnaturally far apart, with muscles like twisting vines or ropes. His feet kicked up small clouds of sand. The dwarf's left hand was thrust forward; in his right hand he clutched a very strange weapon that looked like a long knife, or a short spear the length of a forearm.

A thousand deaths and cities ablaze; the thunder of the cavalry sweeping through deserted streets; love, bitter and beautiful; rivers and cities beheld for the first time; faces of military leaders, courtiers and conquerors – all these events, the stormiest of my heretofore none-too-calm existence, originated in this horrific figure on the sandy path.

Two dark silhouettes emerged out of the fog on the path behind the dwarf: imperial soldiers. Soldiers of the most ordinary kind – not horse guards with peacock feathers on their scale-encrusted helmets, but foot solders in thick dark robes down to their ankles (in the dark it was impossible to tell whether or not they wore armour underneath); in black cloth hats, lined with iron and tilted slightly forward and holding short spears in their hands. They stamped their feet, encased in thick felted boots, boldly. If it hadn't been for the dwarf, I would most likely have lost a few precious seconds and I wouldn't have understood that they were murderers who had stolen into the garden in the dead of night.

Unbelievable! My house in the quiet, lush green quarter of the Imperial Capital was guarded far more vigilantly than many other houses. Two sentries always guarded the gate that led out into the street and behind the second garden was a guardroom, where there was always someone listening for untoward sounds in the night. Guardsmen were permanently stationed at the rear perimeter of the house, by the stables, as well, observing the outer walls.

But now, strange as it may seem, sitting among cushions on a silken carpet in the front garden, surrounded by burning oil lamps and smoking coils to ward off mosquitoes, I found myself to be completely vulnerable. In my left hand I clenched some thick, rough paper – a scroll with vertical rows of sharp black marks that somehow evoked the spring night, filled with the sounds of cicadas and the pungent scent of fresh vegetation.

There wasn't much time to think about what to do next – time, at most, to snap your fingers a couple of times.

Loud hollering was useless – if the intruders hadn't been stopped on their way in, that meant that there was no one there to stop them. It would take much frantic snapping of the fingers for the servants to have time to reach the front garden – and by that time, it would be all over. The hollering itself would take up precious moments I didn't have.

To stand up, turn and run away from the intruders toward the blind wall of the garden was foolish, not only because after that there would be nowhere else to go, but also because the dwarf, like a giant spider, was speeding up to strike a blow.

The only thing left for me to do was to use my opponent's lethal speed against him. That is, I had to draw my feet in their soft leather boots under me and make a leap out of the circle of trembling yellow light and into the saving darkness. Not away, however, but headlong towards the attackers, though slightly to their right, avoiding the iron rod gripped in the Dwarf's right hand. I dashed past his left shoulder and ended up near the left arm of one of the soldiers. The second soldier, though armed with his spear, was momentarily thrown for a loop.

Three jumps and my opponents were already behind me on my left. Not stellar, but pretty good for a start.

The scroll had remained behind on the carpet, but the burning oil lantern was still in my hand. This I flung at the soldier closest to me, hardly daring to hope that it would catch fire. He tried to dodge it, but got drenched in oil all the same. At that moment, I employed one of the oldest tricks in the book, a move right out of a street brawl. I dug my foot into the sand, mid-flight and kicked it into the face of the soldier.

In an instant, all three of my enemies were behind me and I, dazed by the stench of their unwashed bodies, was flying in the direction from which they had just arrived, the direction of the exit from the garden into the courtyard, behind which were the gates to the street, or, rather, to the stone wall that separated the outer courtyard from the garden, toward the old spreading pear tree that grew by the wall and supported its masonry with its branches.

What awaited me in the courtyard – more soldiers and dwarves – I didn't know; but as for the street, now, after the second watch, with the gates of all the quarters of the city long since closed, there wouldn't be a soul in sight. It would have been quite rash on my part to try to escape by relying solely on running, at my relatively advanced age, along deserted streets. The only alternative was to put myself above my adversaries, if not beyond them and then act as the situation demanded.

I grabbed the lowest branch of the pear tree and allowed myself to glance back, risking to lose another second or two.

Pretty bad – the soldiers had already managed to turn their faces toward me, grimacing in the moonlight. The dwarf, his about-face leaving a crescent-like furrow in the sandy garden path, caught up with them and catapulted himself forward.

Masters of martial arts tumble upwards into trees like squirrels. I tried scrambling up through the lower branches, braving thorns, slipping, gritting my teeth and forcing my legs to bend at unprecedented angles under their unexpected burden. My right hand, sticky with oil, almost let

me down, losing its grip. But my foot was already touching the reassuring rough surface of the tiles of the wall; I pulled myself up and turned around.

The dwarf, crouched right under me at the base of the wall, stretched his mouth which was buried in his ropes of beard, into a smirking grin. He gave me no time to consider how to go about kicking him in the head. With his teeth, he seized his sharp iron bar (now I noticed it had a convenient handle) and leapt into the tree.

Next, he flew along the branches like a misshapen black shadow, swinging from one branch to another, propelling himself upward. In a moment he deprived me of my advantage, at the same time taking up a position on the far side of the tree, so that it was between us.

I didn't doubt that he would have the advantage over me, even on the tiles of the wall. I had only one choice – to take him on while he was scrabbling over to me, before he had time to snatch his weapon from his teeth. I would have to try to push him to the ground into the clutches of the soldiers, who even armed with spears didn't pose much of a threat to me as long as I held my position above them.

Slipping down, I began to skirt the tree from behind, stepping on the tiles. The dwarf was already slightly above me among the branches. I had to tilt my head back in order to make out his wrinkled face, which he had painstakingly darkened with soot. Just then he jerked in a strange manner and heaved towards me, twisting his head left and right in irritation. He slithered down through the branches and fell in a shapeless heap right at the feet of the approaching soldiers.

A short arrow with dark plumage protruded from the rags on his back. The soldiers stared dully at him, transfixed.

I had a few seconds to size up the situation and make a move – now I could probably snap my fingers, say, three times.

I stood on the tiled slope of the overhang atop the wall (these tiles covered not only houses, here, but walls alike; walls that divided the city into rectangles like a board game, separating houses and courtyards and the quarters of the city).

While I was here, I was granted a few moments of respite from fear of the soldiers, who were armed with spears, but not with crossbows. But I had no notion of how many enemies were rampaging through my house, how they were armed and what had become of my guards. I knew only that an unknown enemy had materialised in my life and that he had been taken down by an unknown friend. The latter, however, had *also* forced his way into my house, or its grounds, without invitation.

I peered into the darkness, with its massive outlines of trees and the convex ribs of the tiled roofs and walls between them. In the light of the moon, I descried something that astonished me.

A tall, lanky silhouette draped in dark rags stood motionless on the slope of a high roof. A wild mass of tangled grey hair glinted in the moonlight. The figure froze beneath my gaze in a pose that recalled a cat arching its back. It then made a curious, graceful leap sideways along the roof, landing without a sound behind the corner and disappeared from sight.

Was I sleeping, or had I glimpsed the heroine of a hundred urban tales of horror – the grey witch Xiao, who sprang from the rooftops at night and drank the blood of people and horses?

And then it struck me that in the hand of the witch who had just vanished from view was a weapon, one no larger than the sharpened iron bar of the Dwarf. It somewhat resembled a stick, a bit longer than the forearm, the end of which was adorned with a small bow-shaped cross-piece. In short, a crossbow; from the looks of it, one for hunting. A weapon from which you could use effectively with only one hand, albeit from a short distance.

This fleeting glimpse was enough for me. Returning to a house with guards who were nowhere in sight, a courtyard overrun with tramping soldiers armed with spears and grey-haired archers leaping nimbly about on the roof, was not a wise thing to do. As a matter of fact, there was no guarantee that the arrow that had felled the dwarf had not been meant for me, but had strayed a bit too far to the right.

I had to flee.

It takes only a few moments to reload a crossbow. I quickly propped myself up on my elbow on the wall, throwing a quick glance over the tiled overhang at the front courtyard and the gates. As I might have expected, a motionless body lay crumpled in the sand and by the gates, where my oil lamp still glowed, I could make out a second. My guards' lives had been snuffed out without a sound while I sat close by, in a circle of light – and literally at the feet of the grey-haired archer on the roof, who could have read the bold marks of the manuscript over my shoulder, had he wished.

I turned around and moved quickly, then ran along the tiled overhang. I ran, falling repeatedly, banging up my knees, performing awkward little capers – and consoling myself with the fact that the sorry spectacle I made would wreak havoc with the aim of the unknown archer, if, indeed, he had such an intention.

I clambered along the tiles of the wall that separated the outer courtyard from the front garden and sprang onto an adjacent wall that divided my house from the deserted dwelling next-door. I advanced eastward along the wall, in the direction of the Eastern Market of the Imperial Capital.

Running along a tiled overhang, particularly a decrepit, pockmarked overhang, overgrown with grass and occasionally even small trees, wouldn't have been so difficult had it not been for one problem: running along a sloping surface, one leg is always bent at a sharp angle, the body lists to the side and one tends to drop on one's belly every so often, like a load of bricks.

I'm not fat, like most of the Imperial inhabitants, who take pride in a stomach the size of a mountain. But I have lived in this world a surprisingly long time: more than four decades. Most of my peers have already departed from this life or reconciled themselves to the loss of teeth, hair, the flexibility of their extremities, or even their extremities themselves. The God of the Blue Sky was good to me for many years; he had clearly not prepared me for frenzied leaps along the slope of a tiled overhang on legs buckling underneath me.

And still I made my way eastward. Little orange lights flickered between the branches at my feet. Down below, tender strumming on an instrument could be heard; spicy aromas of cooking meat wafted from kitchens nestling in the depths of gardens. Here was a girl, kneeling before a young man at table, pouring him wine from a teapot amidst the blinking lights of the fireflies. Now her young man raised his eyes and was astonished to see there in the dusk a clumsy fellow balancing in the branches, his beard sticking out in all directions, in a soiled dressing gown, western-style trousers and tattered boots. The thick scent of sandalwood from the silent Temple of Teacher Kung. Silk flags fluttering around the oddly angular sides of the mortar of the Temple of Teacher Fo. The columns of the Temple of Fire. Priests shuffle around in their sandals and peer up in alarm at me, rustling in the branches of the trees like a nocturnal bird. Branches and little lights, the pinkish trajectories of bats, the quiet snorting of horses in the darkness. A spring night serenaded by cicadas in a city that no longer exists.

A leap from the wall onto the white sand of a deserted avenue, 130 steps wide. Should I not simply give myself up to the guards, recounting the story of the invasion of my home by robbers? But besides the attacker dwarf, there were two Imperial soldiers who had forced their way into my home. This led me to suspect that an order for my arrest had been issued and, consequently, the circumstances warranted my urgent escape from the capital. If that was the case, I had to report in at our town residence, which was not far (about four quarters away) from my home.

And so – onward.

The shouts of the city guards who seem to have picked up my trail were still faint. I could even reflect a bit on what had happened. The events were similar to those that had led to the death of my predecessor Melek, who had run the purchasing operations of our trading house in the glorious Empire. His guards had survived, however. But they had not the faintest idea how that poor chap, resting like I had been in the garden retreat, had been found the next morning, pierced through the eye with some sort of unknown razor-sharp weapon.

At least now I knew what had transpired. But at the time, my brother and I had no inkling about why it had happened and at whose behest. Melek wrote letters to my brother and me, but there was not so much as a hint about threats to his life, with the exception of the following enigmatic lines: "...strange and alarming news has arrived, which I will occupy myself with in the near future, giving the matter all my attention."

This letter, rolled up, sealed with wax and concealed in a vessel filled with sesame oil, was swaying on the back of a camel, moving at a measured pace along the Great Road to the headquarters of the trading house, when the author of the epistle was already lying motionless, crumpled up on his side in the garden just coming to life, the garden that had now ejected me in such a strange manner.

"Well, who should we send to replace Melek?" my brother asked me soon afterward, sitting next to me under branches hung with ripening golden peaches. "Maybe you'd agree to go yourself? You love the capital. You speak the language of the Empire and even read and write. You're bored here, I know. And when words about 'strange and alarming news' arrive from the Empire, after which the author of those words is killed...well, it's just what you need to spice things up a bit."

That conversation had taken place two and a half years since, but I knew little more today than I knew then.

One last unpleasant surprise awaited me when I was already crawling down from the wall that surrounded the enormous quarter of the Eastern Market, where all the most expensive pleasures of the Imperial Capital were to be found in their most concentrated form. There were few guards here. This quarter (which was, in fact, a city within a city) was guarded by its own inhabitants more vigilantly than any sentry could even dream about. And as I myself was one of the inhabitants, I knew a dark, obscure part of the wall, unknown even to the sentries, where the foundation was old and dilapidated, the tiles were overgrown with grass and weren't as slippery and where the wall was also shaded by an old gingko tree, with its fan-shaped leaves, silver on their undersides and bark like congealed mud. Down the tree I slid, counting on being able to creep from the near side of the wall onto the deserted back-street, where my storehouses of plain white silk were waiting for

shipment to enormous, insatiable Byzantium. But just at that spot under the wall where I had planned on beginning my foray into the city, a character well known to the whole Eastern Market and bearing the undisputedly false name of Udai-Baba (accent on the last syllable) had settled down for the night. A professional holy man – in other words, a preacher of a religion of his own creation – he was perpetually grimy, with tangled hair and beard. True, unlike other prophets of Ind and Baktria, he was absolutely sane and reasonable – one only had to look closely at his crafty eyes, bulging out of his reddened eyelids and turning them almost inside out. Actually, after two or three conversations with Udai-Baba on the theme of eternity, retribution and carnal love as a religious rite, I had a sneaking suspicion that in addition to preaching he was involved in the same, let us say, silk trade that I was. It is, of course, very convenient to be a person who is never required to answer questions about where he is going, where he has been and whom he has been talking to.

This very person was leaning against the base of the wall just now, when I had crawled down and landed almost literally on his stomach. I bore a closer resemblance to a holy man than did Udai-Baba at that moment – I was impossibly filthy, my face scratched and glistening with sweat, hatless, my hair strewn with twigs and bits of dirt. Udai-Baba stared with his bulging eyes as I landed on the soft earth and subsequently attempted to stand up on my legs, which buckled clumsily under me.

Now everything became much easier. It would no longer be necessary to keep glancing backward and upward to make sure I wasn't being pursued by a grey-haired archer. I had no doubt that she could easily have caught up with me with her flying leaps. And since she hadn't tried to, it meant she was in fact my saviour and not my enemy.

Here, at the market, it smelled like smoldering coals and the coagulated juices of smoked meat. Garbage collectors moved here and there, weaving in and out like shadows. Here, a rag-tag Sogdian hobbling on stiffened legs and covered with dirt would raise no eyebrows – anyone would suppose he was a caravan trader who had already had one too many teapots of wine before dark and had just woken up in a ditch.

And so, with my last drop of strength I reached our town residence, where, as always, the oil lampions burned and visitors who had decided to while away the night here reclined on carpets.

At the gates, hefty fellows with faces normally devoid of expression, but now full of alarm, intercepted me. It seemed that everyone knew all the details of what had happened to me even before I had arrived. The strongmen led me out underneath a sheltering tree hung with illuminated lanterns. My dear Sangak hastened toward me, beaming with a smile boasting a paucity of teeth, which somewhat unnerved people who didn't know him. He watched as I was settled on carefully prepared rugs and pillows, then snapped the fingers on his only hand, his armed raised above his head.

The yeasty smell of a jug of warm beer wafted up under my nose. As soon as I had drunk to the bottom in one long draft, the jug seemed to melt away and soft feminine hands (at least two pairs) began to stroke my neck, my face and even the crown of my head with towels of the softest muslin soaked in warm ginger water. The drops meandered in little rivulets under my collar, which was ticklish and devilishly pleasant "Soon there will be enough warm water for a tub, my lord," Sangak said quietly, without a trace of emotion, his immobile inky blackness obscuring the moon above me. He now looked like a rhino from the Imperial Zoo that had been captured in the shallows of the Great River – with his thick column-like arms, bald head between two mobile ears and tiny eyes. Sangak lacked only a horn above his nose for the resemblance to be complete.

The situation was a delicate one, for Sangak's responsibility at the trading house was to ensure that I was not visited at night by dwarves bearing sharpened iron rods, accompanied by two soldiers from heretofore unknown regiments. Recent events should have leveled a terrible blow at his professional pride, to say nothing of the fact that his fate and his possible demotion to lowly caravan trader, now hung on my words.

And that was the mildest possible outcome. But my massive friend knew well that I wouldn't make such a decision without long deliberation and therefore he conducted himself with dignity, though not without compunction.

"I'm sorry I woke you, dear friend," I said humbly. "You've probably had a hard day."

"I wasn't sleeping, my lord," Sangak answered. "I was thinking."

"About the imperfection of this world?" I asked, settling myself more comfortably against the warm trunk of the tree.

"I was thinking about the sheep," sighed Sangak, continuing to stand, waiting for the gesture from me that would allow him to sit down. Receiving it, he perched on the edge of my rug at an angle that revealed his face, tenderly clasped the stump of his left arm with his right hand and continued:

"I was thinking about why, of all the beasts in our world, the sheep is so wonderful, why mutton is prized more highly than any other meat. It doesn't turn into mush between your teeth like the meat of some small-sized bird and it doesn't break into thick sinews like beef. It's just right for the teeth and tongue. And the aroma! But where can I find the aroma of real mutton, the kind we're used to at home, the kind I constantly dream about here? What's wrong with the mutton in this accursed city? Why is it that the best that they can do with mutton here is to treat it like the Inda people do?

"To steep it in sour milk with ginger and garlic overnight? And then cook it in clay for hours?"

"Exactly right, my lord," Sangak confirmed, still speaking with the same cautious restraint. "And, by the way, although I know your habit – not to eat much at night, still, if you want anything, anything at all, including pilaf, the whole kitchen is awake and awaits your orders...but I suspect, I'm even completely certain, that you will wish to have..."

"Fruit," I requested. Sangak at once snapped his fingers again, his armed raised over his head like a dancer from Damascus and a moment later my nose basked in the scent of a real Iranian melon that had managed to survive the winter. It would literally have swum in its own juices if it had not been packed in pieces of ice. Sangak had

yet again salvaged his reputation.

"You can imagine, Sangak my friend, that things other than mutton have occupied my thoughts on this night," I began, signalling the transition to serious matters. "But I see that you were forewarned about my arrival, since you had time to see to the cutting of a melon..."

"Bukar raised the alarm when he saw the murdered guards – two at the gates and one in the sentry box near the kitchen," Sangak reported dispassionately.

"He couldn't find you anywhere at home. He sent someone on horseback to me here. I immediately sent the 'wisemen' to your house. They have already arrived there, I think and are hard at work. In the meantime, I thought about it a bit and decided that if you were forced to stay away from home for some reason or other, you would either take cover somewhere until morning or show up here before then. And if something worse had happened, it would be necessary to go to the city guards in the morning. But I gave orders based on the most auspicious scenario. And I reinforced the watch here at the inner and outer perimeters. The sentries advised me soon that you were coming on foot through the ceremonial square...Bukar is also here."

"Well, let's talk to Bukar then."

Sangak again snapped his fingers over his head with a dancer's flourish and the figure of my temporarily vanished guard materialized out of the shadows and came over to our tree by the wall. His grey hair glinted metallically. Like Sangak, he knew me well and didn't waste time trying to justify himself, but waited silently for my questions.

"Forgive me for causing you so much trouble tonight," I said. The derision in my voice made Bukar's face, greyish in the moonlight, go white. "Let's begin from the beginning. What exactly did you hear? What made you come out to look?..."

"A rustling, master. From somewhere up above," the warrior answered after a short pause. "It seemed that someone was on the roof enclosing the front garden. And then something louder, footsteps and stamping – also up above. I first ran out to the sentry box, where I saw Aspanak lying face down and he was bleeding.

Then I ran to your bedroom, where I didn't find you and then people approached along the road and ran to the gates..."

"Through the front garden?" I questioned, interrupting him.

"Yes, master."

"And what was in the garden?"

"Nothing," Bukar replied, pausing again. "Though it clear you had just been there. Your manuscript was lying there, the lamps were burning, it was smoky...and there were tracks on the path. Many. I avoided them."

"Go on."

"Then I went up to the gates and saw two dead men. Vgashfarn and Devgon."

"How had they been killed?"

"Vgashfarn by a long, sharp lance through the eye," Bukar said, trembling almost imperceptibly. "Like Aspanak in the sentry box. But Devgon – his neck was broken. That's all."

"What do you mean 'that's all'? You didn't see any more dead men? Or anyone at all?"

"No. No one."

"No one at all? Strange...so, that's all you have to report?"

"Almost, master....We began searching for you all over the house. And when we didn't find you, I jumped on a horse and rode here, through the city, as fast as the wind. The guards didn't even try to catch up with me. They don't have horses like that."

But I read some sort of doubt in Bukar's eyes.

"What else did you see, friend?" I prompted him encouragingly.

"You won't believe me, master...but this rustling on the roof...naturally, I turned my attention to the roof after this and I saw...I glimpsed it above the tiles on the edge of the roof, the one that faces to the east..."

"It...what was it?"

"It wasn't a person," Bukar murmured quietly.

"What was it then? Did the tigers escape from the Imperial Zoo?"

Bukar sighed heavily and remembering that I like facts and not premature conclusions, he answered:

"A shape. Not a man, not a woman. It jumped along the rooftop. Long grey hair. A black face. It

didn't move like people move. I saw it only for an instant. It was going towards the east, along the roof-tiles.

Sangak exhaled noisily and became perfectly still, waiting for my reaction. He was well aware of what I thought about the demons, spirits and devis my people were given to seeing. Or the witch, Xiao, known to all the city.

"How did she move?"

Bukar, after thinking a bit, dropped down on all fours and tried to execute a strange sideways leap.

There could be no doubt: he and I had seen the same thing.

"Thank you, my dear Bukar," I said presently. "You have acted altogether honourably. We will talk again. And I am very sorry that your friends and mine have lost their lives."

Bukar hesitated a bit, as though he couldn't believe his luck, then let out a deep sigh and deftly made his exit. Sangak, painfully aware that no one had told him "you have acted altogether honorably," kept silent.

"Well now," I said, ready to draw some conclusions. "Bukar heard me running on the root-tiles. Everything that happened before that occurred in virtual silence. This is very curious. To destroy three warriors without a sound – this is beyond... First, of course, they killed Aspanak in the sentry box. The dwarf did this singlehandedly. He crept over the roof, fell onto his neck from above and went right for his eye."

"The dwarf!?" Sangak exclaimed, his eyes widening.

"It would be very unpleasant for you if you were to meet up with him, I assure you...Then he crept up to the gates and gave a signal to the soldiers. When armed soldiers knock on the door, it doesn't arouse suspicion, but it provides a serious distraction. The guard strikes up a conversation and at that moment the dwarf sneaks to the back...Vgashfarn and Devgonare killed at the same time, so they don't manage to utter a sound. The dwarf kills one of them with his strange weapon; one of the soldiers kills the other. That means that he knows how to break someone's neck in the wink of an eye... also curious. In fact, this is why the soldiers were necessary. The dwarf couldn't have done it on his own. And, by the way, they weren't soldiers at all. And all the time I calmly sat in the front garden; maybe I heard a slight commotion at the entrance, but... that's what gates are for – for people to knock on, asking for directions, or asking for food. Completely ordinary events and sounds... To continue, Sangak. The dwarf's body disappeared. And the "soldiers" disappeared. That means they removed it. Moreover, in record time. And they vanished without a trace. After my escape, there was nothing more for them to do in the house, where a hue and cry was already starting up.

"Ah, you killed the dwarf!" Sangak exclaimed, with obvious relief.

I didn't want to disappoint him; I didn't tell him about another strange fact – that the grey-haired creature on the roof had set out, judging by Bukar's story, toward the east. But I had fled in the same direction. Then followed the logical question: why had this creature not caught up with me? Especially since my progress during the flight eastward along the walls was not aided by youthful vigou,r.

"And so, Bukar ran out into the garden when I had already left and the dwarf had already been removed," I continued.

"But how can that be, if the blockhead saw you all the same and mistook you for the witch Xiao on the roof?" Sangak protested.

"I truly hope that he wouldn't make the observation "neither a man, nor a woman; not a person at all..." in regard to me," I remarked, shaking my head. "No, up there on the roof was someone else I saw with my own eyes; otherwise I wouldn't have fled, Sangak. And he or she had a crossbow....In short: at daybreak, let the 'wisemen' explore all the roofs; what's more, let the guards from this day on learn to keep watch over what transpires there, above their heads. And – thank you, Sangak. The melon was delicious.

My friend, understanding well that the final judgment on his blunders and his accomplishments was still to come, relaxed a bit.

"Your room is ready," he said in a low voice, treading beside me. "The tub with hot water should be ready by now. The bench is spread with fine imperial linen, just as you like it. You will need

a massage now and one in the morning; all the same, after such an adventure, your whole body will ache, believe me... it's too bad that you cannot give a massage to yourself – all of us who have had occasion to experience your hands on us are luckier than you are..."

Afterwards, having almost fallen asleep in the tub, they literally had to carry me into the room where I had spent numerous happy nights during my former visits to the capital, before I began to manage all our trade activities here. I started to recall stories about the dreadful old hag Xiao, springing over the roofs on moonlit nights. And at the next moment the sun was shining – not early morning, but bright midday sun; and meek Sangak personally handed me something soft and warm, a slightly sagging parcel wrapped in a fine cotton tea-towel, from under which escaped the most wonderful smell in the world – freshly baked bread from the tandoor oven. By my bed stood a bowl full of large ripe translucent mulberries.

.

LEV DANILKIN
GAGARIN – MAN AND MYTH (EXTRACT)

Translated by Andrew Bromfield

Chapter 5

Having once escaped from the Earth's gravitational pull, on his return Gagarin naturally found himself back in its power and he felt it just like everyone else. But the unique status that in reality was his for only one and a half hours was miraculously prolonged: in the eyes of virtually the entire population of the planet he remained a body free of the influence of earthly gravity. As if, from being a simple citizen of the USSR, he had been transformed into its satellite, a kind of Moon that had broken away from the Earth, famously provoking the irrational interest of quite ordinary people who could not possibly have been less concerned with the problems of conquering space.

It is not clear exactly who first decided that on the evening following "the dawn of the space age", Gagarin should go travelling and pay a few visits but, in any case, all the countries of the world started vying with each other to invite him to come and see them. What exactly motivated them to send these invitations? Was it the idea that, since he had already flown over their territory anyway and could have seen any secret facilities there, they might as well invite him over on a more neighbourly basis? And what did they actually want from him? The most plausible answer to that question was given by a rapturous Cypriot gentleman who almost went down on his knees in the middle of a London press conference to beg a favour of the Russian major: "We will kiss our Gagarin if he comes to Cyprus". Ah yes, at bottom that was what they wanted, nothing more: to kiss the "son of earth" who had made "a flight to the stars". "Our Gagarin." The question was, how far did this justify the issue of an exit permit to "our" – ah, yes, nonetheless OUR 27-year-old Soviet major, who had flown to the stars, but had not sprouted his political flight-feathers yet?

There is nothing surprising about the fact that the propaganda machine exploited Gagarin to the hilt to represent its own interests within the USSR and its satellite states; or that his first trip, made literally only a couple of weeks after his return to earth, was to Czechoslovakia, followed by Cuba,

Poland, Hungary and so on: this was a well-planned "lap of honour", a promotional road-show organised according to a straightforward model. But could our cosmonaut be allowed to exit his pre-planned diplomatic orbit and enter a distinctly hazardous "meteorite belt"?

Those who trusted to luck and authorised Gagarin's first, less minutely controlled, initial sallies into the "genuinely foreign" (i.e. "capitalist") world, apparently did not know themselves what dividends to expect – but they decided it was worth the risk of floating a redesigned ideological product at a moment when the political markets of the West were in a volatile condition (Britain was losing one colony after another; the USA was not yet fully prepared to take on the role of global policeman, which had previously been played by Britain and, in addition, the Americans were not sure what to do with a wildfire practically in their own backyard – Cuba). Essentially, with Gagarin, Soviet propaganda offered a world that was going through a global political crisis – the West, The USSR's own allies and non-aligned countries – a kind of open platform. The concrete significance of the USSR's ability to fly faster and higher than all other countries was not entirely clear (most probably some kind of military superiority) – but what was clear was the possibility of jumping on the bandwagon, chummying up, being friendly neighbours, concluding economic agreements and so on. The effect that followed the launch of this "platform" exceeded the very boldest expectations. Gagarin became the Soviet authorities' most successful PR project of all time, allowing them to continue their political expansion from space into the territory of other states. The subsequent response of these opportunists was primarily not one of satisfaction, but boundless surprise. The stunned Soviet official Kamanin noted in his diary: "Observing the crowds of millions acclaiming Gagarin so passionately, I frequently recalled my youthful impressions of a popular print showing Jesus Christ meeting the people. My memory had retained the radiant face of the Divinity in the centre and fifteen or twenty astonished and questioning faces in the background".

Subsequently explanations of the following kind became popular: Gagarin's visits to the West were a kind of cover operation for the USSR's political activities that didn't make such good political PR – the erection of the Berlin Wall, the attempt to install rockets in Cuba. In hindsight, perhaps, this account appears to correspond to the reality, but in May and June 1961 nothing of the kind was required. A "Soviet" explanation is probably more plausible (in this case the country in question is Brazil, but that is not important): "A country that is extremely dependent, both politically and economically, on the USA wished to demonstrate its own significance by receiving a Soviet peace ambassador". (16)

Anyone who ponders Gagarin's life realises sooner or later that he actually has to think through, not only the biography of the man, but also the "biography of the idea". Strange as it may seem, this "idea" is not identical with communism. When all of a sudden, out of the blue, the Soviet Union was transformed for a while from Mordor into a beacon of global good, it wasn't because everybody suddenly took such a great liking to the idea of communism. The world was presented, not only with the marketable product of a highly competitive system, but with something else as well. The "idea" that "genuine" ("capitalist") foreigners saw behind Gagarin could be described as the glamour of space – and the glamour of red. Which, you must agree, is not exactly the same as communism.

Gagarin's odyssey of 1961-1962 was documented in detail by Soviet journalists who focused on the propaganda aspect of the visits (since, after all, that was what they were paid to do). Three entire travelogues were published on the basis of the material produced: *Good, Good, Gagarin!* (the cry – in Russian – with which Gagarin was greeted in Japan), *The Orbit of Friendship* and *First Citizen of the Universe,* by N. Kamanin. All three publications are undoubtedly documentary instances of the usual rhetorical format of the period, but their usefulness as a source for Gagarin's biography is limited. For instance, mention is made of the fact that Gagarin was greeted at Tokyo airport by a crowd of thousands, but nothing is said about the group of ultra-rightists, also present, who were roaring "Gagarin go home!" through a megaphone. But then, who would have thought the author would let slip, for instance, that very late in the evening, when it was impossible to do any more work anyway, Gagarin accepted an invitation from "Arab friends" "to visit the music hall 'Under the Pyramids'." Naturally, any description is going to be extremely meagre, punctuated by ritual provisos ("'We didn't come here to have a good time, but to work,' said someone, reminding us of the words Yuri had spoken: 'Time is for work, with an hour for fun. Let's go'."). But the fact remains that we do learn Gagarin went to a performance by "the famous dancer Hoda Shams el Din, who danced for about an hour and danced with astonishing grace and elegance". (17) A few observations can be found in Kamanin's diary (fortunately for Gagarin and unfortunately for us, he did not go everywhere with the major). Something is revealed in the reminiscences of members of delegations of various kinds, in which Gagarin was often included – although on occasion the Soviet witnesses are clearly inclined to exaggerate the hostility of the context: thus, in describing the situation at the Helsinki Youth Festival of 1962, the secretary of the Komsomol Central Committee, S.P. Pavlov, paints an entirely Boschian picture: "Drunk, yelling, chewing gum, they flung stones, bottles of Coca-Cola and dead rats at the festival buses. They howled like real demons, jerked about to the twist and rock'n'roll and shouted 'Heil Hitler!'."(23) Far more interesting, however, is the view from the outside, the opinion of disinterested observers. And since, inside the USSR, foreigners were only allowed anywhere near Gagarin with the greatest reluctance, the only way to learn the opinion of disinterested observers is to study the foreign press coverage.

Gagarin's played his first away game in Czechoslovakia, at a time when that country was a satellite of the USSR, so the sceptics have good reason to write off the reported enthusiasm of the public to exaggeration by the official press, or claim that it was artificially inspired by the authorities, who wished to ingratiate themselves with the USSR. Let us accept – although there is good reason to doubt the fact – that in the spring of 1961 every radio speaker in Czechoslovakia was playing the song "Dobry den, Majore Gagarine" ("Good day, Major Gagarin") and he was not swamped with carnations tied up with ribbons, but with lilac, which the Czechs had simply picked for themselves. Gagarin's most exhausting, essentially nightmarish, journey was to India and Ceylon, during which he met Nehru and Indira Gandhi, visited Bollywood and spoke in public 18 times a day in a temperature of 40 degrees Celsius, when he was "sucked dry" (his own words) and not rewarded for it in any way ("I never even saw any elephants in India," he complained to Kamanin). The most grotesque journey, even judging only from Soviet witnesses' reports, was to Western Africa – Ghana and Liberia: unfortunately, however, the sources are limited to propagandist literature, which is not all that interesting. So, for "total immersion" we have selected a different journey, one that was short, but the most striking of all in terms of drama. An exemplary, model journey.

To England.

Firstly, this journey is better documented than all the others by various mass media, not only the pro-Soviet ones (for some reason, in fact, the Soviet newspapers did not place any particular emphasis on it; in some strange way, everything said about England in *The Road to Space* seems to be forced out through clenched teeth; for most of the incredibly boring five pages Gagarin retells his own replies at the press conference, which he thought were good.).

Secondly, the visit to England was made in "combat conditions". Britain is a curious case of a country that has never demonstrated excessive enthusiasm for outsiders, especially if those outsiders arrive in the uniform of a competing military bloc. In view of England's inherent scepticism concerning the technological achievements of others (this is essentially an irrational prejudice against other people's ideas, a complex known in social psychology as NIH – Not Invented Here), it was hard to be certain that space would astound the country. And finally, England had Fleet Street, with its means of obtaining information and ways of presenting it that have not infrequently been described as tinged with yellow. These would seem to be the ideal conditions for the moment of truth: a sober-minded and wary audience, a brazen press, prepared to hound the very devil himself, pragmatically disposed politicians – now they'll surely take out their very biggest magnifying glass and tell us who this vulgar vocational school graduate really was!

The context of this trip? On 25 May Kennedy gave his historical "moon speech" in Congress, demanding the allocation of 531 million dollars during the next financial year to prepare for putting an American astronaut on the Moon. No one had any doubt that this was an unscheduled appeal – and it was clear who was really dictating the agenda at that moment. Indeed, no room was left for doubt: "These are extraordinary times. And we face an extraordinary challenge ... It is a most important decision that we make as a nation. But all of you have lived through the last four years and have seen the significance of space and the adventures in space and no one can predict with certainty what the ultimate meaning will be of mastery of space."

By the way, Gagarin was supposed to visit France before England, but the authorities there (or, rather, the *Syndicat de l'industrie aéronautique*) withdrew the invitation, when they realised that that the cosmonaut would be in Paris at the same time as Kennedy and took fright, not so much at the unforeseen consequences of this proximity, as at the wrath of America (as the Russian newspaper *Izvestiya* rightly pointed out: What are they afraid of – that the public's attention will be attracted to the wrong man?).

The trip to England failed to go to plan right from the very start. Naturally, it was possible to count on a warm reception – within the limits of traditional English xenophobia and snobbism of the English. But to foresee that, three months after his flight, a Soviet officer would be greeted, in a foreign country that was a member of a competing military and political bloc, with almost greater enthusiasm than in his homeland? That crowds of people would wait to welcome him along the road from Heathrow and swamp him with bouquets of flowers – just as they did along Leninsky Prospect on the way from Vnukovo airport? That women would faint in ecstasy at the sight of this visiting representative of the USSR?

Much vaunted Fleet Street, with its inherent immunity to overly warm emotions, also behaved like an organism incapable of generating political antibodies to the Gagarin infection. The first round had effectively already been lost in Moscow. In early June 1961, Gagarin was yanked out of the Black Sea resort of Sochi to meet with Burchett and Purdy, two Australian journalists who had been given the go-ahead for an exclusive interview with "the most inaccessible man in the world". A certain Moscow scientist told them in jest:

"Well, if it was Khrushchev, I'm sure you wouldn't have had any problems. He talks to journalists every day. But this Yuri Gagarin..." and he shook his head. (3)

Nonetheless, they were lucky: Gagarin was preparing for a visit to England and it was regarded as politically expedient to let him talk to journalists. On the basis of their conversation and other materials they had collected, they promised to publish a whole book in England, a book to answer one of the most important questions on the world's mind in 1961: Who is Mr. Gagarin?

"It was his first and only meeting with western journalists on a face-to-face basis. The only thing separating them was the table."(3) The setting for this meeting looked very promising, but it can only be described as a journalistic fiasco. The Australians didn't manage to get anything intelligible out of Gagarin – not even any vivid reactions that no one else had recorded before. With nothing to show for their pains, like all the rest of their colleagues, Burchett and Purdy merely bleat about the incredibly bright blue

eyes, the disarming smile and – a roll of drums for an astounding intimate detail! – a mole on the major's left cheek, instead of clarifying what any normal western journalist would have asked about: Why did he lie about the precise way in which he landed, how did he feel about the unmasking of Stalin's personality cult and what did he think about the possibility of sex in space?

In essence, the same thing happened with Fleet Street itself: it succumbed to the same hysteria as the newspaper-buyers. Yes, of course, the English press observed the cosmonaut closely and tried its very best to uncover some aspect of his behaviour that did not correspond to the official dossier. Yes, they did observe that Gagarin was very short, that his hair was too shortly trimmed (for some reason they had shaved his temples almost naked immediately before the trip), that he applauded himself all the time, which was strange: however they were unable to dig up anything more criminal than complaints about his hand hurting after thousands of handshakes. The attempts to probe the depths of the cosmonaut's psychology – his "soul" – were even less impressive; the conclusion that can be drawn from these intense observations can hardly be called original: He is a man of the heavens, not of the earth. And you really do get the feeling that they regard him as an alien from space – humanoid, but not entirely human.

We can only guess at what was going on inside Yuri Gagarin's head during these meetings. It might seem to the outsider that the "work" he performed during his "second orbit" was no more demanding than his "activities" during his first. All he had to do was ride in an open car in all weathers, wave his hand in greeting, smile into the camera, accept all sorts of original gifts (anything from household electronics to a car), demonstrate a sound appetite (after all, they fed him not just from the heart, but with ingenuity: Vostok salad, Rocket soup, Orbit roast, Gagarin gateau and Yuri ice cream – that's the actual menu from San Paolo and we can be quite certain that the Brazilians were by no means original), occasionally change into national costume (in Liberia the natives dressed him up in a striped robe, set a hat made of feathers on his head and stuck a spear in his hands, telling him to hold on to it tight), repeatedly reproduce mechanically, but with feeling, one and the same story about his flight, maintain the bare minimum of genteel small talk – and, well, kiss the girls, in whom he inspired a positive torrent of uncontrollable feelings.

In actual fact it was much, much more than that: it was being an icon.

We must realise that he was not prepared for this job. It was one thing to be the object of an indigenous Russian cult; he could discuss the peculiarities of that situation with Budyonny, Voroshilov and Maresiev. It was quite another to undergo conversion into a different currency and become the embodiment of a cargo cult for the circumspect and sceptically inclined western public. Possibly he was trained to be a hero, possibly he was even briefed on how to improve his manners by some Professor Higgins of Moscow– but no one explained to him how to be a pop star and a Hollywood celebrity. And who was there in the Soviet Union to explain that to him? Kamanin, perhaps? It's one thing to stand on the mausoleum beside Stalin or Khrushchev, waving your hand and quite another to make conversation with the Queen of England and Brigitte Bardot. Who could they have hired as a consultant to explain how to answer when he was told: "The president of the US was here a month ago but ten times as many people have come to see you". Or when a girl pointed at him and squealed in ecstasy: "Ooh, he's got a shaving cut on his cheek!" Elvis Presley? Marlon Brando?

This rock star life was a kind of weightlessness too – an environment as ill-suited to a Soviet citizen as space itself; and naturally, Gagarin was obliged to tumble about in it and sometimes hold very awkward poses. What saw him through was his high tolerance of stress – much higher than the average – which allowed him not to recoil too obviously from the glaring flashlights. High stress-tolerance and the ability to adapt to complex circumstances. He could compensate for his ignorance of foreign languages with his perpetual smile, for his lack of high society graces with his discreet gallantry: his awkwardness at finding himself in an unfamiliar situation was usually smoothed over by unpretentious political

humour ("Taking up the small, smoothly planed sticks that serve the Japanese as spoon, knife and fork, Yuri Alexeevich joked: 'The finest weapon in the world!' [13])

What he was not good at was answering questions. His press conferences – which we shall discuss later – produced a depressing and risible impression. At a pinch, he could just about deliver a talk on a set topic (usually "My flight and its significance for the party and the government"), or make a five-minute speech larded with a monstrous number of ideological and pseudo-futurological clichés ("The time is not far off when inhabited ships and laboratories will fly into space and to other planets of the Universe and as well as Russians in the crew there will be …" – what came next depended on which capital city he happened to be in at the time). But at press conferences he often had to answer specific and frequently deliberately awkward questions – and Gagarin was disastrously bad at dealing with thatBut nonetheless – as the Russian saying goes, "simplicity outdoes robbery" – he doesn't get embarrassed and carries on regardless, even if his technique is clearly inferior to his opponents'.

Stress-resistant, certainly, but there were far more stress factors than we could imagine. What sticks in his memory out of the insane whirligig of that first day in London? "A woman with pink hair." Ye gods.

On the other hand, we should realise that his surroundings were by no means as hostile as we assume now, extrapolating the present situation to that period. Kingsley Amis had a novel – not read by many people nowadays – called *Russian Hide and Seek*, which describes England under Russian occupation: totally run down, mired so deeply in barbarity and ignorance that the English are even forgetting their own language. Strangely enough, the only ones who try to maintain them in a civilised state are the officers of the Russian occupation forces – who are more like the noble officers in *War and Peace* than barbarians. Of course, this is a grotesque satire, in which everything is back to front – but it is also a novel indicative of the psychological context in which Gagarin found himself. Gagarin did not come to the West as a poor relative who was lucky to have been invited to this great feast of life, but as a representative of a great power – a power with its own, perfectly competitive culture and also a power with too many people within reach of its nuclear arsenal. Moreover, in the early sixties, the West did not see the USSR as "Upper Volta with rockets", it was more a matter of "The Soviet Juggernaut". The USSR was a "fashionable" country, an opinion-maker among nations, which could certainly not be said of Britain itself – the Britain that was in the grip of a severe identity crisis (this is the period characterised by Dean Acheson's sarcastic remark: "Great Britain has lost an empire and has not yet found a role"). The Britain that had realised the colonial system was collapsing before its very eyes and, therefore, the habitual model of development and economic growth was no longer fit for purpose. The Britain that was inclined to provoke its ally, America, which seemed too rich, too vulgar, too surfeited, too self-confident and too arrogant. Gagarin's arrival was an excellent pretext to make the point that, if Britain wished, she could find other partners – more amenable and more polite. And the Russians had a good front man – better than the Americans, with their tedious astronaut Shepard and the good-looking, but slippery Kennedy, associated in people's minds with the mafia, FBI and CIA.

It should be said that, as the visit proceeded, high-ranking officials and the British establishment, who had sanctioned the trip, suffered ever greater discomfort and confusion. And no wonder – imagine if in 1961 an American NATO officer had come to Moscow (well, all right, London's not New York, say – to Kiev) and suddenly found himself greeted by crowds carrying flowers. Should we forbid the public unrest? Ask 'who's last in line' and practice a wider smile in front of the mirror? In this sense the step taken by the queen, who sidestepped all the regulations and invited the Soviet officer to her palace for lunch, should be recognised as exceptionally farsighted. But then, in later times she would also demonstrate that she is a resourceful woman: the example of the flowers that she laid on the people's memorial to Diana, whom she deeply despised, illustrates this same

character trait of Elizabeth Windsor.

Gagarin in England is a play in which the main character is Gagarin, but it is first and foremost about Britain, which suddenly found itself in quite exceptional circumstances; a play in which the action feels strange to both parties.

* * *

Herald Journal
Newspapers throughout the world last week were filled with the sickening spectacle of Great Britain as she publicly prostituted herself for the benefit of Communism's newest hero, spaceman Yuri Gagarin. The spectacle has been a slap in the face of Uncle Sam and the people of the world who are dedicated to the preservation of freedom. (42)

The *Daily Mirror* wrote: "This morning at 10.30, Major Yuri Gagarin arrives in London. Gagarin is a brave man. He is also the symbol of the greatest scientific feats ever achieved." (53)

Francis Spufford, *The Red Plenty*
This was the Soviet moment. It lasted from the launch of Sputnik in 1957 through Yuri Gagarin's first spaceflight in 1961 and dissipated along with the fear in the couple of years following the Cuban missile crisis in 1962. (It was already going, in fact, at the time of the 1964 election; it was a piece of Wilson's appeal that was premised on a fading public perception and was dropped from Labour rhetoric shortly thereafter, leaving not much behind but a paranoid suspicion of Wilson among egg-stained, old-school-tie spooks.) But while it lasted the USSR had a reputation that is now almost impossible to recapture. (52)

It became known on Friday that he would come to England. Yesterday, after doubts about what the procedure for meeting him ought to be, the British government finally decided who will welcome the world-famous hero, who we will send to welcome Gagarin on behalf of the entire British people when he gets off the plane. He will be met, not by the Prime Minister Macmillan, not by the Foreign Secretary Lord Home, not by the Minister of Science's Office Lord Hailsham, but by Francis F. Turnbull (Secretary of the Minister of Science's Office – N.K.) The explanations offered for this consist in the fact that Yuri Gagarin is not a head of state. But no one believed that Yuri Gagarin was a head of state. However, it remains a fact that he has accomplished a heroic feat which dwarfs anything that Macmillan or any of his ministers have ever done … (53)

On Tuesday 11 July the plane with Yuri Gagarin on board arrived at London's Heathrow Airport. (53)

Exactly three months to the day after his flight in Vostok I (48)

Alexander Soldatov, Ambassador of the USSR to Great Britain
When there was about an hour left before the Soviet plane landed and we got into the car to drive to the airport and meet Yuri Alexeevich, the Queen of England's Private Secretary phoned and asked me, on the queen's behalf, whether, in our opinion, Major Gagarin could accept an invitation to lunch at Buckingham Palace, on Friday, 14 July? We replied that, in our opinion, he could, but we would give a definitive reply immediately after Yuri Alexeevich's arrival in London. (54)

Time
Crisp and smiling in the olive drab uniform of a Soviet air force major, Yuri Gagarin bounced out of an Aeroflot turbojet at London Airport to help publicize Moscow's Trade Fair and all Britain gave him a tumultuous welcome. Thousands lined the 14-mile route into London for a look at the world's first cosmonaut, (44)

Since friends of the Soviet Union published the plan of Yuri Gagarin's route from the airport to the Soviet Embassy in the *Daily Mirror* newspaper for several consecutive days, the population of London had the opportunity to line up in advance along the itinerary followed by our cars. (54)

Thousands lined the 14-mile route into London for a look at the world's first cosmonaut, cheered

and chanted "Gagarin" as his motorcade swept by. Standing in an open silver Rolls-Royce with a specially issued license plate "YG-1," Yuri waved and grinned. (44)

Oleg Kudenko, *The Orbit of Life*
The number plate attached to his brand-new open-top silvery Rolls-Royce was: "Y.G-1" ("Yuri Gagarin – the First"). Journalist acquaintances of mine told me later that a special vehicle identification number had only been produced once before – for the arrival in London of the new American president, Kennedy. (17)

Tom Wolfe, *The Right Stuff*
Over the three weeks since the great Soviet triumph of Gagarin's flight, one terrible event had followed another. The United States had sent in a puppet army of Cuban exiles to conquer the Soviets' puppet regime in Cuba and instead suffered the humiliation that became known as the Bay of Pigs. This had nothing directly to do with the space flight, of course, but it heightened the feeling that this was not the time to be trying brave and desperate deeds in the contest with the Soviets. The sad truth was, *our boys always botch it*. (6)

The Miami News
Yuri Gets Blonde's Number (27)

A curvaceous blonde singer let it be known today that Soviet spaceman Yuri Gagarin was riding around London in an automobile with her license number.
The Soviet cosmonaut was driven around yesterday in a Rolls-Royce with special plates numbered YG-1. "YG" for Yuri Gagarin and the "1" for the first man in space.
But "YG" also stands for Yana Guard, a bosomy blonde who sings under the name Yana. And she acquired the YG-1 auto registration five years ago for five pounds ($14) from the previous owner as a publicity gimmick.
When she saw photographs of the Gagarin welcome, she promptly got hold of a reporter and asked, "What's he doing with my registration number?"

The official purpose of Gagarin's visit to London was to visit the Soviet Trade Fair and the idea to ride him around behind YG-1 plates came from James Brewster, whose firm is doing publicity for the fair. Brewster refused to comment on the purloined number except to say that he does not represent Yana.

The London Country Council's Auto Registration Authority, which approved the number for Gagarin, was embarrassed.

"Everything was done in such a hurry," said an official. "The number isn't a London one at all. It is a Yorkshire County number. There seems to have been a slipup."

Yana, who used the registration on three previous cars, now uses it on her $11,000 Mercedes sports auto. She was not annoyed about Yuri using her number – or about the publicity for herself.

"I think he's a wonderful and courageous man," she said. "I would love to meet him. Then we could decide who has the best claim to the number.

"I only hope the police don't take his number, or they'll come looking for me." (27)

When he turned into Kensington High Street, the crowd broke through the police barriers to surge into the street. Watching 100 yds. away behind the fence of Kensington Palace, a lone figure waved: Princess Margaret, who had waited half an hour to glimpse Yuri. (44)

The first cosmonaut had absolutely no idea that in turning towards the jubilant masses he was being "not entirely" gentlemanly. Princess Margaret and two of her close aides had been waiting for forty minutes in continuous rain for the hero to appear, but he took no notice of her. After all, she was on the side dominated by mansions and palaces. (13)

It should be said that Princess Margaret was no stranger to space technology. For instance, on 18 March 1960, she had visited Britain's Jodrell Bank Observatory and transmitted a signal via the radio-command link to the interplanetary station Pioneer-5. The response signal was received 25 seconds later, after covering a distance of 1.67 million km, establishing a world record for remote space communications at the time. (62)

All day, while the press conference was going on at the Soviet Trade and Industrial Exhibition in Earls Court ... (53)

Ottawa Citizen
...a trade fair - reciprocating the recent successful British exhibition in Moscow and aimed at picking up as many immediate orders here as possible (47)

Models, human and plastic, would seem to be the latest Soviet gimmick in the peaceful co-existence competition.

The slinky blonde ones, dressed in the latest fashions from the Central Fashion House of Moscow, trip neatly and light-heartedly along the viewing ramp twice a day at Earl's Court viewing hall, clearly the hit of the first Soviet trade fair to reach England. (47)

Ga-Ga Over Gagarin.
Ladies' man Yuri Gagarin, who flew solo in space for the Soviet Union, finds himself surrounded by Soviet models during visit to a Russian exhibition in London. (32)

...this huge exhibition […] is the largest ever held by the Soviet Union outside the country.

And the message they bring, according to Soviet officials, is that this is a complete picture of Soviet life in the new Russia, land of the future.

And compared to the permanent Exhibition of Economic Achievement of the USSR, opened two years ago in Moscow to show visitors and the natives the progress of the Soviet Union, this London trade fair reveals almost capitalistic excess in expenditure and a clearly bourgeois flare in design and layout.

This appeal to the monumental is thus the cue for entry into the main or Cosmic Hall, where the visitor takes off into outer space. Aside from Major Yuri Gagarin, his space ship, the Vostok, seems to be the sun around which the universe turns as it swirls up into the domed ceiling of Earl's Court. (47)

Times

Behind him, as a testament to space worship, a model sputnik tottered dangerously on its plinth and it took half a dozen men to keep it from falling. (29)

Francis Spufford, *The Red Plenty*

Give your imagination permission to engage with some unlikely facts: in the 1950s, the USSR was one of the growth stars of the planetary economy, second only to Japan in the speed with which it was hauling itself up from the wreckage of the war years. And this is on the basis not of the official Soviet figures of the time, or even of the CIA's anxious recalculations of them, but of the figures arrived at after the Soviet Union's fall by sceptical historians with access to the archives. The Soviet economy grew through the second half of the 50s at 5%, 6%, 7% a year. As Paul Krugman has mischievously pointed out, the USSR's growth record in the 50s elicited exactly the same awed commentary as Chinese and Indian growth does today. Admittedly, "growth" did not mean exactly the same thing in the Soviet context that it did in, say, the American one (average for the period 3.3% a year) or in the British one (average: 1.9%; have a stale crumpet). Soviet growth was counted differently, was biased massively towards heavy industry and did not necessarily imply a matching growth in living standards. (52)

It is only when you get into sections dedicated to atomic power plants, synthetic rubber plants ...
Fashion show. The latter is not soon likely to worry Dior or Balmain, but it is the nicest visual evidence that Soviet clothing has finally begun to graduate from the overall and drabness of beige. (47)

At a press conference in the Trade Fair's fashion hall, so many Yuri fans crashed in that Fleet Street newshawks, among the world's most agile and aggressive, barely got in any professional questions. (44)

Following Gagarin's comprehensive account of Vostok's flight and the problems resolved during it, British scientists presented him with two volumes of the scientific correspondence of Isaac Newton and a photograph of the radio telescope at Jodrell Bank, which had followed the Soviet spacecraft's flight in orbit round the earth. Yuri Alexeevich, in turn, presented Howard Flory, the president of the British Academy of Sciences, with a book of his autobiographical notes, *The Road to Space*, thanked him for the books and remarked warmly: "They are especially dear to me, because the flight into space was achieved in accordance with the laws of the earth's gravitation, first discovered by the hero of British science, Isaac Newton." This allusion to Newton, so appositely linked with the latest achievement of Soviet science, delighted the scientists. (9)

While Yuri Gagarin looked round the exhibition, thousands of Londoners jostled outside the exhibition building. The only ones who could get in were the small number of fortunate individuals who had managed to obtain tickets the day before. The English people's eagerness is understandable. Once inside the exhibition at Earl's Court, they were immersed, as it were, in Soviet reality. Naturally, the space exploration hall attracted special interest, with its model of a starry sky under the dome. Young people and people of the older generation all strained eagerly to hear the voice of the presenter, telling the story of how Soviet man was making his way into space. And how many questions they asked the first cosmonaut when he spoke at the press conference! (53)

Instead, Yuri tactfully fielded such inane queries as whether he has nightmares (answer: no). (44)

No, he never had anything like that. He slept quite normally and he had never been much of a dreamer, anyway. (43)

Alexander Kamshalov in *Gagarin's Immortality*, ed. Yuri Ustinov

Soon we went off to sleep. And suddenly there was a bloodcurdling scream. Yuri came running in, pale and frightened, in just his underpants;

at first he couldn't even explain anything intelligibly. "Yura, what happened?" I asked. He kept repeating over and over again, as if he was struggling to get the words out: "Bats, bats" and he pointed upwards and at his own body. We went to his room and turned the light on: it was calm and quiet, nobody there. There was a crumpled sheet lying on the floor. And only then did he tell us what had happened. When Yura turned out the light, covered himself with the white sheet and tried to get to sleep, hundreds of bats, so he said, started swooping at him, they grabbed at the sheet, at his hair, it was terrifying ... But when we entered the room and switched the light on, there wasn't a single bat there, the windows were tightly closed and there weren't any cracks or holes in the walls. Where had they got to, had he dreamed the whole thing? He couldn't stay in that room any longer, and we went to mine. He confided to me: "You know, I'm more afraid of bats than anything in the world, they're unpredictable and there were lots and lots of them". (16)

When Gagarin explained that he might visit Poland and Cuba next, a little man leaped on a chair to shout: "We will kiss our Gagarin if he comes to Cyprus."

A woman asked about using women for space exploration. Yuri, his blue eyes twinkling, was all gallantry: It might be useful, since "a woman's appreciation of beauty is more developed than that of a man. If a flight seems beautiful to a man, it would seem even more so to a woman." (44)

Nikolai Nosov, *Dunno on the Moon*
Miga answered all the questions, and it must be said that he did this most resourcefully, that is, when it was possible, he answered the question directly, when he didn't know what to say, he replied evasively, but not once did he say "I don't know". For instance, when one of the correspondents asked how long the cosmonaut would stay in their city, Miga replied:
"As long as necessary."
When asked if he would visit other cities, Miga said:
"Yes, if he wishes to."

When asked if the cosmonaut had any intention of purchasing any goods in their city, he replied:
"That will depend on what goods we are able to offer him."
There were so many people asking questions that poor Miga started losing patience and barely managed to stop himself being quite rude to someone. (18)

How did he feel about becoming a celebrity? "I am still an ordinary mortal. My gold star, Hero of the Soviet Union medal, bears the number 11,175. That means 11,174 people accomplished something very notable before me." (44)

Mr Kruschev [sic], for example, had three Gold Stars and was a hero of Soviet Labour. (43)

N.N. Denisov, *Good, Good, Gagarin!*
One of the many questions asked at the press conference ... was this: Who is the most important leader of all the work on studying space in the USSR? "Nikita Khrushchev," Gagarin declared to general applause. "We Soviet cosmonauts call him the pioneer of the space age." (9)

Khrushchev simply adored him. I recall that Yura once asked me to go with him to some function where the "big-shots" had got together. Nikita Sergeevich was the only one who was late. And then he came in, handed his hat to someone and straight away, paying no attention to any of the Politburo members, he dashed across to embrace Gagarin. (62)

Major Gagarin won over the crowds from the moment yesterday afternoon when he walked jauntily across the red carpet at Earl's Court, holding a large bunch of gladioli. The crowds chanted "Yuri, Yuri", the major smiled disarmingly and one woman, delighted to find a touch of human fallibility in the hero of space, cried out: "He's cut himself shaving" (29)

Before the mob scene was over, a dozen women had swooned under the combined impact of the crush and Yuri's sex appeal. (44)

One girl, braver than the rest, broke though cheering autograph hunters to plant a kiss on Gagarin's sunburnt cheek. Said 23-year-old Olivia Brayden: "Now I have made history by being the first English girl to kiss him. I made up my mind as soon as I saw him that he was my new No. 1 heart-throb." (45)

The Southeast Missourian
A pretty British dental nurse kissed Soviet spaceman Yuri Gagarin Wednesday night and pronounced him "the most kissable man in the universe."

"Oh, it was wonderful, just wonderful," said Olivia Brayden, 23. "I'm mad about him. I shall remember it always."

Olivia ambushed the 5-foot-5 Russian as he emerged from the Soviet Embassy on his way to a reception. She flung her arms around his neck and gave him a solid smack on the cheek.

Yuri, a married man whose wife remained in Moscow, looked embarrassed.

So did his Soviet bodyguards. They grabbed the girl and pushed her back into the crowd gathered to see the spaceman.

Gagarin – who was kissed on both cheeks and the mouth by Soviet Premier Khrushchev after his space flight – quickly recovered his composure. He smiled, climbed into the car and rubbed at the lipstick on his cheek with his handkerchief as the car pulled away.

"Yes, I have a boyfriend," Olivia told newsmen, "and I don't think he's going to like it very much."(30)

Herald Journal
Gagarin is really nothing more than a soldier of Communism. That he would be willing to dump a hydrogen bomb on the free world with pride for the "cause" does not matter perhaps to the British.

That he would force the enslavement of the young British nurse who in her childish enthusiasm planted a kiss on his face should not be considered perhaps. (42)

Said columnist Winifred Carr in the Daily Telegraph: "This perception about us is the most appealing thing about Maj. Gagarin. When we turn a man into a hero, it is not enough for him to be brave, good-looking and good-natured. Being women, we also like to think he appreciates us as well."

Olga Franklin, a Russian-speaking reporter for the Daily Mail, found Gagarin made her feel "like a queen."(45)

Major Gagarin is the spaceman with sex appeal. The girls interviewed by the cameras could not have been more dewy-eyed and enthusiastic about even Elvis Presley or Marlon Brando. (26)

Like Gagarin, Lindbergh was a fresh-faced, boyish figure with modesty and a disarming upturned grin [...] But considering that the Russian achievement was a deadly serious part of the propaganda war, Yuri Alexeyevich has managed to invest it with a surprisingly Lindberghian casualness and grace. (45)

What made British girls go gaga over Gaga? In his three-day visit to London, the Russian spaceman Yuri Gagarin set more hearts a-flutter than Charles Lindbergh did in 1927.

Housewives and bobbysoxers mobbed him in the streets. (45)

... literally swept the English people off their feet, not to mention the English girls, who even ran out of the hairdressers' salons in their curlers and greeted him happily: Yuri! Yuri! (54)

The hottest-selling souvenirs were colored postcards of the cosmonaut. Any woman reporter who attended the press conference on his arrival was asked by friends: "Did you find him attractive?" (45)

...Roddy has a flash of inspiration.
'I know!' he says, seizing upon a pedal car and squeezing himself with difficulty into the driver's seat. 'I'll be Yuri Gagarin, and this is my space-car and I've just landed on Mars.'

For like every other boy his age, Roddy worships the young cosmonaut. Earlier in the year he was even taken to see him when he visited the Earl's Court exhibition and Mortimer had held him aloft so he could actually shake hands with the man who had voyaged among the stars. Now, crammed awkwardly into the undersized car, he starts to pedal with all his might while making guttural engine noises. 'Gagarin to Mission Control. Gagarin to Mission Control. Are you reading me?'

'Well who am I supposed to be then?' says Hilary.

'You can be Laika, the Russian space dog.' (5)

When I wrote the novel *What a Carve-Up!*, I needed to find some event that was important for a boy born in the early 1950s. And it seemed to me that the most obvious thing was to make his hero Gagarin (64)

A near-exhausted Major Yuri Gagarin went to bed last night after a welcome by Londoners which left him with a hand painful from hands-shaking. The 27-years old Soviet cosmonaut went to bed at the Russian Embassy "nursing an aching right hand" after he shook hands with more than 2000 people. After 70 minutes of hand shaking and balcony waving at the first reception Gagarin went upstairs to his bedroom for a bath and a lie down. (34)

He skipped his last appointment in a jam-packed day – a dinner at the luxury Dorchester hotel given by businessmen trading with Russia. A spokesman at the Soviet embassy said: "Major Gagarin is tired and has gone to bed."

But soon after 10p.m., the cosmonaut left in an official car with three companions, followed by another Embassy car with a party of fashionably-dressed women inside. It was announced: "Major Gagarin and the ladies are going dancing after a tour of the West End."

The spokesman added: "It would be more than my job is worth to tell you who he is with and when and where they are going to dance." (36)

Major Gagarin spent over an hour touring central London. … Nobody recognised him during his tour. At 11.15 his car swept back to the Russian Embassy where a spokesman said: "Major Gagarin is enchanted by London at Night." (36)

The Times
A welcome that sometimes bordered on hysteria (29)

Nikolai Kamanin, "Fliers and Cosmonauts"
… I shall take the liberty of using the expression: "immersed in an ocean of universal adoration". Let me remind you that in the early 1960s, no individual on the planet was more popular than Gagarin. (15)

Then a tall, gaunt middle-aged individual with his shirtsleeves rolled up to his elbows appeared beside him. He held out a piece of paper to Yuri Alexeevich and said:

"Please, Mr. Gagarin ... Please, an autograph ..."

With a movement that had become habitual, Yuri Alexeevich took a pen out of the inside pocket of his uniform jacket in order to apply his signature. But when he looked more closely at the greenish piece of paper that had been handed to him, he shook his head. "Nou," he said. "It is dollars ... nou autograph."

The man with the rolled-up shirtsleeves was an American who was staying in the Britannia Hotel and the piece of paper he had held out for an autograph was a hundred-dollar bill. Many foreigners before that had asked Gagarin to sign on their identification documents or on money. But Yuri Alexeevich had stuck to his principles and never done this.

"Yes! It's a hundred dollars ..." the American jabbered delightedly when he heard Gagarin speak English. "Please autograph ... It's verry good!"

"Nou, nou," Yuri Alexeevich replied even more insistently. "It is verry bad!" he tore a clean page out of his notebook, signed it, added the date and handed it to the American, together with the hundred-dollar bill. The American was not pleased with this turn of events. He looked regretfully at Gagarin, thinking that he did not understand the significance for its owner of a hundred dollar bill with Gagarin's signature, put the money back in his wallet, bowed stiffly and headed for the exit. (9)

Valentina Gagarina, *108 Minutes and a Whole Life*

We fly to England. We land in London. A warm reception at the airport ... After that it's like a merry-go-round. A press conference, the presentation of the British Interplanetary Society gold medal, a conversation with Lord Droyd about the benefits of breast milk in raising a child ... Everyone wants to see me, touch me, slap me on the shoulder. My arm is actually tired from all the greetings ... At a reception I saw a woman with pink hair ... (11)

Yu. A. Gagarin was invited to visit the Union of Foundry Workers of England. (20)

On his flight from London to Manchester Major Gagarin for a few minutes held the controls of the British European Airways Viscount air liner, "Sir Isaac Newton" (33)

Exactly three months to the day after his flight in Vostok I had ushered in a new age of space exploration, the trim figure of Yuri Gagarin strode down the gangway of a British Viscount airliner and walked briskly out across the runway of Manchester airport towards a sea of expectant faces and flashing camera bulbs. Heavy banks of cloud had obscured the aircraft's final descent and a ferocious downpour had lashed the tarmac, soaking the top hats and tails of the waiting dignitaries. However, what the rain could not dampen was the warmth of Gagarin's smile and the raw enthusiasm of the crowds who thronged the concourse: pushing at the safety barriers and seizing every vantage point in an attempt to catch a glimpse of their hero. (48)

On a visit to Manchester in a driving rain, Yuri took one look at the waiting crowds and insisted the top be kept down on his Bentley convertible for the drive into the city. "If they can stand in the rain," he said, "so can I." (44)

But as soon as Yuri saw the cheering crowds gathered at the very first street corner to welcome him, despite the rain, he asked that the car be stopped and the top pulled down. "If all those people," he said, "are getting wet to welcome me, surely the least I can do is get wet too!"

We arrived at the headquarters of the Foundry Workers Union wet to the skin, or "wet to the bone", as they say in Russian, but warmed by the truly remarkable enthusiasm of the British people's welcome for the world's first cosmonaut, the first man in space. (51)

The presence of the Soviet air officer gave Manchester its most exciting day in years. Swarming crowds knocked down Gagarin's interpreter and almost swept the spaceman off his feet. (28)

Small children dressed up in home-made space suits and stayed away from their lessons in order to wave at him from street corners. Teenage girls crowded the platform constructed for him at Trafford Park and surged through the police lines which surrounded Ringway airport and the union offices at Brooks Bar, anxious to obtain an autograph, to present a bouquet of flowers, or to steal a kiss. Seasoned factory workers rushed to shake his hand or to slap him on the back, stumbling over their words of praise, while outside their training ground the United team broke off their practice to wave at the "Magellan of the Cosmos".

After the drab years of post-war austerity, there seemed something almost magical about the first human being to have broken the bounds of the earth and viewed 'through the portholes [of his spaceship] ... a diamond-field of shining, bright, cold stars'. Mary McClellan, who had travelled up to the rally at the Metrovickers plant that morning, thought that in contrast to the grey suited businessmen and the dark overalls of the factory workers Gagarin cut an 'unbelievable' figure in his bright green uniform; and that he looked as though he had been filmed in 'technicolour, thrown into a stark contrast by the monotone which surrounded him'. (48)

When they heard about this, many English people cancelled trips of various kinds in order to stay at home and see the first cosmonaut.

Then there was the meeting with thousands of workers at the Metropolitan-Vickers plant.

They say that before the meeting started, Yuri Alexeevich was taken to the foundrymen and he asked them to let him carry out a melt, in breach of the programme of the visit. The English foundrymen had misgivings about the cosmonaut's idea, but Gagarin managed the melt successfully, winning the approval of the acknowledged masters of their trade. (20)

The Amalgamated Union of Foundry Workers presented him with an honorary membership medal inscribed "Moulding Together for a Better World." Replied onetime Metalworker Yuri graciously: "I am still a foundry worker at heart." (44)

As both the product and expression of all that was best in the mature Soviet system, he seemed to represent the embodiment of the new 'Socialist Man' and delighted his audience at the union offices by declaring that he was 'still a foundryman at heart'. Presented with the honorary membership of the Foundry Workers' Union and a medal bearing the hopeful inscription 'Together moulding a better world', Gagarin paid tribute to 'a union which ranks among the oldest in the world and has such fine traditions', before wishing its members 'every success in... championing working class rights and interests and working for a world of peace.

These sentiments were expanded upon during his address, later in the day, to the workforce at the Metro-Vickers factory: then the largest industrial plant in Western Europe. Skilfully circumventing many of the most intransigent problems created by the Cold War, Yuri stressed the need for arms reduction and peaceful co-operation in pushing forward the boundaries of science and technology and in pursuing a policy of understanding the detente. He explained that 'Although only one person was aboard the spaceship, it took tens of thousands of people to make it a success. Over 7,000 scientists, workers and engineers just like yourselves were decorated for contributing to the success of the flight' and concluded to the sound of thunderous applause that 'There is plenty of room for all in outer space ... I visualise the great day when a Soviet

spaceship landing on the moon will disembark a party of scientists, who will join British and American scientists working in observatories in the spirit of peaceful co-operation and competition rather than thinking on military lines'. (48)

The ceremony ended with the singing of for he's a jolly good fellow.' After the ceremony the weather cleared and several thousands shouted "We want Yuri" until he appeared at the office doorway.

After the visit ended Major Gagarin was entertained at a civic lunch at the Town Hall. He met Professor Bernard Lovell. Major Gagarin praised the great help Professor Lovell had given Soviet scientists in the tracking of satellites and space rockets – "a fine example of the scientific co-operation in the peaceful conquest of space." (33)

In 2009, in an interview for BBC TV, Bernard Lovell claimed that KGB agents had tried to kill him. According to him, in 1963, during a visit to the Crimean Radiophysics Observatory, he was irradiated with a powerful beam of electromagnetic radiation. According to him, the details of the unsuccessful assassination attempt are described in a document that will be published after his death. Lovell links the attempt to his work in Britain's military programme. The radio-telescopes at the Jodrell Bank Observatory, where the scientist worked, would have played a key role if World War III had started. Their antennae could pinpoint the launch of Soviet rockets, making it possible to launch a counter-strike. (58)

... The Soviet cult of cosmonauts was popular, not only within the country, but also in the international arena [...] They were the jet-propelled envoys of the Soviet global charm campaign and since they carried with them the good feelings of their country, they attracted the attention of the whole world. (12)

Nikolai Kamanin, "Fliers and Cosmonauts"
After the meeting, Major Gagarin was invited to Manchester town hall. The cars moved slowly.

There were tens of thousands of people standing on all the pavements.

At the central entrance to the town hall building a military orchestra played the Anthem of the Soviet Union. Mr. Biggs, who had donned his gold chain for the occasion, invited his guests to lunch. Even in this the Mancunians had decided to distinguish themselves. Lunch was served on the "coronation service". (15)

N. Kamanin, 'A Citizen of the Soviet Union'
Lunch was served on the "coronation service", worth five thousand pounds sterling. (53)

Although Whitehall chose to remain aloof, the situation in Manchester was very different. Gagarin's visit to the city had been organised in advance, under the auspices of the local trades councils and had received the blessing of the civic leaders who were only too happy to organise a lavish reception for him at the Town Hall. As the rain cleared, the Red Flag fluttered beside the Union Jack over Albert Square and a brass band struck up the national anthem of the U.S.S.R. to welcome the arrival of the first cosmonaut. In an age before the Beatles, when rock music stood on the flimsiest of foundations and the role of the pop singer was still ill-defined, the first man in space was guaranteed a status normally reserved for visiting royalty and Hollywood film stars. The young Martin Kettle [a future star journalist at the Guardian] plastered pictures of Gagarin on his bedroom walls, while in the pages of the Times one correspondent captured the feelings of many, for whom 'space-men have been the wildest fiction', the stuff of popular novels, comic books and radio programmes until suddenly 'one morning, this fantastic fiction' had become scientific fact. Who, he asked, 'would not...walk a few hundred yards to see this incredible' man, who 'visits us and talks to us. (48)

Later the well-known English public figure Konni Zilliacus would say: "Those who believe that our country is inhabited by reserved, cold people who are not inclined to make a show of their feelings should have been with us when Yuri Gagarin visited England. He could have followed Julius Caesar in saying: 'I came, I saw, I conquered'." (21)

If Gagarin's popularity with the people of Manchester was undeniable, then the nature and long-term political significance of his visit was still in doubt and was to be hotly debated over the course of the next few weeks, in the pages of the local and national press. Commentators, from both the left and the right, were agreed that the tour had done little to alter the domestic political landscape, to remove deeply held prejudices, or to prompt a thorough-going reassessment of Britain's Cold War alignment. However, the prestige of the labour movement as a whole and the Foundry Workers' Union in particular, had been greatly enhanced by the presence of the youthful cosmonaut. Gagarin was a potent symbol of the power of organised labour and socialist thought. (48)

... A brief flight, and Yuri Gagarin is back in London again. (13)

In the meantime, the British popular press, which spent Monday agonizing over whether the British government would give Gagarin a VIP welcome or not, is giving him a "Hero of the United Kingdom welcome" at least. (24)

Alexander Soldatov, Ambassador of the Soviet Union to Great Britain
... a rather interesting fact and rather typical of the atmosphere in England then. Late one evening, I was informed that an elderly woman, already a grandmother, was waiting for comrade Gagarin at the embassy. She had come from Wales with her grandson in order to present Yuri with a bundle containing her family valuables, since she did not want these valuables to go to the fascists in a future war! She wished these valuables to be used for the cause of strengthening peace. We fed the old woman and her grandson and tried to persuade to go back home with their valuables. (54)

The Palm Beach Post
An 11-year-old cockney boy, dressed in a

space suit, waited for him outside the Soviet Embassy during a stop off in the afternoon. When the Russian asked the boy his name, the lad answered: "I'd better not say. You see, I played truant from school to get here." Laughing, Gagarin signed the boy's autograph book. (35)

We didn't have much time at our disposal. We decided to devote it to looking round the city. (13)

Yuri Alexeevich was interested in everything and he used every minute to see and learn as much as possible [...] In the Museum of the History of London, among the showcases with the coronation robes of the kings and queens of Great Britain, he spotted a modest case with items relating to the Russian ballerina Anna Pavlova lying under the glass [...] a cast of her foot and a white ballet skirt with a large precious stone.
He visited Hyde Park and Kensington Gardens. Recalling a film that he had liked, WaterlooBridge, he visited that rundown, quite unremarkable bridge. (8)

It had been assumed that early in the morning, before the tourists came flooding in, the excursion would pass off relatively calmly. But it was not to be! The historical Tower of London, that ancient castle, which had only recently become a unique museum, was literally besieged by young people and schoolchildren. (13)

The expectation of peace and quiet was disappointed. A thunderous outcry: "He's coming!" shook the air the moment the car with the red pennant appeared. It was a while before we could get into the fortress. Even Fieldmarshal Lord Alexander, who was supposed to greet the guest at "the Queen's House" was powerless to force his way through the rows of excited, shouting people. Mounted police also failed to help. (53)

At one point he became a prisoner in the grim Tower of London because of the press of people. (35)

Then the visit to the town hall. The Lord Mayor of London, Sir Waley-Cohen, solemnly welcomed the Soviet hero at the "Mansion House", located in the northern district of the City. (53)

He was received by the Lord-Mayor of London, which brought to a halt all work in the City offices, as everyone poured out to cheer the guest. "It's a great privilege for the City of London," the Lord-Mayor said at the reception, "to entertain one of the great pioneers of mankind." (51)

Before meeting Macmillan, the astronaut was guest of honour at a luncheon given by the Fellows of the Royal Society for the Advancement of Science.
"He was quite ready to reply to our questions," said Prof. W. H. McCrea, president of the Royal Astronomical Society. "He did not stonewall (beat around the bush) and spoke spontaneously.
"The fellows were most impressed by him. He was able to answer questions in a way which only someone who knew about his subject could have done. He is a very good observer."
Asked what question he put to the spacemen McCrea answered:
"I asked him about the clouds he saw on his flight."(35)

Said Prof. Bernard Lovell, director of Jodrell Bank, Britain's radio telescope:
"The major discussed technical matters in technical language. You can tell he's the product of an extensive educational program in Russia."(35)

Somewhat later, Gagarin was received by the prime minister of England, Harold Macmillan. This meeting had to take place, because the English people had already expressed their respect and admiration for the Soviet cosmonaut. (53)

The sheer scale of public enthusiasm for the visit, which came at the height of the Cold War, had elsewhere caught the authorities by surprise. The Macmillan government, which had initially been reluctant to invite the cosmonaut to Britain, hastily added an extra day to his schedule and offered a grudging official sanction to what had originally been conceived as a trades union-sponsored tour, aimed at promoting economic co-operation between the East and West. (48)

Macmillan asked the cosmonaut several general questions, enquired how he was feeling, invited him to look round the office and admire the views from the windows of the apartment. Yuri Alexeevich had brought the English prime minister a present – a signed copy of his book *The Road to Space*. On behalf of the government of Great Britain, Harold Macmillan presented the Soviet cosmonaut with a silver salver made by English craftsmen. The sixty-seven-year-old head of the English government accompanied the twenty-seven-year-old cosmonaut to his car and said goodbye to him warmly. (53)

'Leadership and Change: Prime Ministers in the Post-War World – Macmillan'
Afterwards, Gagarin was driven down the Mall to see Macmillan at Admiralty House, where the Prime Minister was then living whilst Downing Street was undergoing renovations. The Foreign Office came up with a special Rolls Royce, registration number YG1 and Gagarin drew vast crowds, waving Union Jacks and Russian flags, as his cavalcade with outriders made its slow progress through the cheering throng. London was en fete. Macmillan watched the noisy spectacle from an upper window in Admiralty Arch. "Of course," he observed to John Windham, "it would have been far worse if they had sent the dog!"(49)

REUTERS
YURI: A DELIGHTFUL FELLOW SAYS MAC. Macmillan described Soviet spaceman Major Gagarin as a "delightful fellow" after a 20-minute private talk with him at Admiralty House. The Prime Minister presented the Russian with a silver salver as a memento. (38)

Flight
Acknowledging our applause in the Soviet manner by applauding in return. (43)

Gagarin, who had endured the traumas of wartime as a child, inspired trust as a "peace envoy". His genial expression contradicted the stereotype image of ferocious, fiendish Russians. With his youthful jollity and vivid style of presentation, he was able to charm people and win them over in every country. (12)

Gagarin was invited to a reception arranged in his honour by the English minister of aviation. Minister of State J. Emery, Air Marshal Ronald Lees and other high-ranking officers of the Royal Air Force congratulated Yu. Gagarin. Many famous English pilots, air commanders and figures from the world of aviation were present. In the general discussion, which was conducted in a friendly atmosphere, our rec ord-holding pilots were mentioned and due acknowledgement was paid to the achievement of Soviet aviation. The course of the discussion made it clear that the fame of our Tupolevs, Iliushins and Antonovs, which had been shown in the air parade at Tushino on 9 April 1961, had reached as far as England.
The conversation was about flying and the conquest of space. But not only about that. Every now and again they veered onto the most important, most topical subject – peaceful coexistence. (53)

Nikita Khrushchev's speech at a reception in the Kremlin, 9 August 1961
Anyone who says that is clearly afraid, but we do not want war. We have been through it all. We did not submit when the Germans were outside Moscow; when they reached Stalingrad, we did not submit. So do you think if Adenauer tries to frighten us with his Bundeswehr, we could just put our hands up? We can say to him: If you organise an attack on us, the German nation will cease to exist in this thermonuclear war. These bombs will be detonated on German land. We will do everything to defend ourselves. We'll try to use them, we won't hold them back. (7)

The attempts of some to hide behind phrases like: "We are soldiers and our job is to obey orders, not to think," appeared naive. When

English pilots were fighting off attacks by the German Junkers, they didn't just carry out orders, they thought about something, didn't they? Yes, we were friends in wartime, when we had one common enemy. Why should we quarrel in peacetime? Now only madmen do not understand what war is.

"We have a strong air force," the English fliers said in conversation with Yu. A. Gagarin.

"Russian fliers know how to flight. And our aviation technology is very advanced. And ... rockets. And ... in general ..." (53)

Nikita Khrushchev
We have said that we have a bomb equivalent to a hundred million tonnes of TNT. And this is true. But we won't detonate that bomb, because even if we detonate it somewhere as far away as possible, we could still smash our own windows. And so for the time being we will hold back and not detonate this bomb. (57)

Such comments are pleasing to us, but we are talking about something else, about the fact that our peoples can come to terms on everything without brandishing the bomb. (53)

At the Air Ministry reception the Secretary of State for Air, Mr Julian Amery, presented the non-smoking major with a silver cigarette box and received in return a copy of Maj Gagarin's new book on his flight into space. (43)

When Gagarin visited England in July 1961, there was much talk in Cabinet about the appropriate level of royal hospitality. Should it be a state banquet at Windsor? But Khrushchev in 1956 had only been given tea at Windsor. Perhaps a visit to the Queen Mother at Clarence House? The royal diary was very full at the time and it was a sudden request. Finally, Gagarin was invited to one of the Queen's regular Buckingham Palace lunches, fellow guests including Bud Flannigan of the Crazy Gang and Lord Mountbatten. (49)

"Forward to Buckingham Palace" - with those somewhat mischievous words and with his by-then already world-famous grin, Yuri reminded us that the time had come for the main event of his visit to Britain"(51)

He was welcomed in accordance with a solemn ritual laid down two centuries earlier. It was the changing of the guard: guardsmen in gold tunics and tall hats of bear fur switched places, horsemen rode about impressively.

The grand entrance began with a broad staircase, flanked by narrow staircases, on which the people greeting us were standing, with a perambulator containing the Queen's son Andrew.

Gagarin and his companions were led to a small sitting room. Lord Mountbatten, Chief of the Imperial General Staff, turned to Yuri Alexeevich and said:

"I'm a man of years now. I've seen a lot in my time and many things that I have gone through or experienced will remain in my memory all my life [...] But there is one event that made the deepest impression of all on my memory and I am proud of it. It was in my distant childhood: the Queen of Great Britain held me in her arms [...] Andrew will also remember for the rest of his life how he saw the world's first cosmonaut from his pram." (20)

Alexander Soldatov, Ambassador of the USSR to Great Britain
As if emphasising the great importance that they placed on Yu.A. Gagarin's trip, the queen said that for the first time in history the royal family had allowed all the servants and court officials to line up in the hallway, so that they could welcome Yuri Alexeevich. Lord Mountbatten asked me if I had noticed a child in a perambulator on the right flank of the ranks of servants and emphasised that it was the queen's youngest son, Prince Andrew, because when Andrew was an old man, the queen wanted him to be able to say with pride that he had seen the first cosmonaut in the world. (54)

N.N. Denisov, *Good, Good, Gagarin!*
In the reception hall, with its huge carpet in pale-pink tones and windows overlooking a park neatly trimmed in the English manner, about twenty ladies and gentlemen were already waiting for us. Each of these people muttered his or her name as they shook Gagarin by the hand, but I must admit that neither we, nor Yuri Alexeevich,

remembered them. What point was there? It was clear enough anyway that they were members of London's upper crust, accorded the high honour of seeing the Soviet cosmonaut, not somewhere out in the street, but in the royal apartments. (9)

The Queen had made up her guest list for the luncheon before she learned of Yuri's visit to London. (36)

There were three of us who accompanied him to that memorable lunch at the Palace with the Queen: the Soviet Ambassador Alexander Soldatov, Lieutenant-General Nikolai Kamanin, who was at that time in charge of the cosmonaut unit and I, his interpreter (51)

The other guests included the comedian Bud Flannigan, the head wardress of the largest women's prison in Britain (Mrs. Joanna Kelly) and the leader of the climbing expedition that had conquered Everest (Sir John Hunt). While waiting for the hostess of the reception to make her entrance, we sipped moderately on the drinks handed round by the footmen, exchanged meaningless phrases with those present about the weather, the beauties of London, the notable sights at places where we had already been. (9)

"Just then, without any warning, a pleasant-looking middle-aged woman entered the room, dressed very simply, without any jewellery or traces of makeup – it was the Queen of England. Walking beside her were her husband, Prince Philip and her ten-year-old daughter," writes Kamanin. (20)

But then the butler swung the side door wide-open and announced in a loud voice: "Her Majesty Elizabeth the Second". [Strangely enough, Helen Mirren, the actress who played Elizabeth II in Stephen Frears' film The Queen is Russian in origin – Elena Mironova: and not only is she Russian, she's from the Gagarin District of the Smolensk Region.] (58)

Everything went quiet. But some people there were unable to suppress a smile. First a small, paunchy dog of some undistinguished-looking breed appeared in the doorway. It ran into the hall on its short legs, sniffed at the air briskly, snorted, then spun round on the spot and sat down facing the door, as if it was waiting for its mistress and indicating with its entire posture that everything here was in order. (9)

Lewis Carroll, *Alice in Wonderland*
Alice was rather doubtful whether she ought not to lie down on her face like the three gardeners, but she could not remember ever having heard of such a rule at processions; 'and besides, what would be the use of a procession,' thought she, 'if people had all to lie down upon their faces, so that they couldn't see it?' So she stood still where she was and waited.
When the procession came opposite to Alice, they all stopped and looked at her, (4)

"How do you like London and its inhabitants?" the queen asked her Soviet guests.
"Until now I had always judged the English from the novels of Dickens and Galsworthy," replied Gagarin. "To me they always seemed aloof and impassive. But here we have met people with open smiles and warm hearts."
"You're right," remarked Elizabeth. "There are fewer and fewer Forsytes. Different times – different manners." (10)

Alexander Soldatov, Ambassador of the USSR to Great Britain
Prince Philip enquired about a few technical details, in particular how the structural stability of the space craft was maintained. (54)

Pot Luck at Palace for Yuri... but Boris the interpreter may go hungry (31)

Alexei Leonov
In 1961 Italy awarded him a decoration. And he took me with him to the embassy on Vesnin Street. Gilded candelabras, curved feet on the furniture, everyone bowing ... Yura gives a speech. And that was the first time I heard words like: "Ladies and gentlemen!" And further on – "Honourable Mr. Ambassador!" He had never

been in an embassy before! My jaw dropped, it was all so fine and beautiful! Then he walked up and kissed the ambassador's wife's hand. "Yurka, where did you get all that from?" I asked. He laughed: "I read it in *Consuelo*." Later the English queen also wondered where he could have got an education like that. (55)

To get round the occasional speechlessness of her subjects when confronted with their sovereign the equerries would sometimes proffer handy hints as to possible conversations.

"Her Majesty may well ask you if you have had far to come. Have your answer ready and then possibly go on to say whether you came by train or by car. She may then ask you where you have left the car and whether the traffic was busier here than in – where are you from?" "long-standing lines of inquiry – length of service, distance travelled, place of origin". (2)

... the Queen asked Gagarin:
"Will a girl fly into space in the Soviet Union?"
"Definitely," replied Yuri Alexeevich, "we have complete equality."

They had their photo taken as a memento, which according to etiquette, the Queen was not supposed to do. She explained to the journalists:
"I have been photographed with a man of the sky, not the earth, so I haven't broken any rules." (13)

"Yuri Alexeevich did not know how to use the cutlery," said one of the journalists. "All the lords kept glancing at Gagarin curiously to see what he would do with it. The cosmonaut realised this and said to them: "Let's eat Russian-style". He took the biggest spoon and put some kind of salad on his plate with it. The Queen, as a well brought-up lady, said: "Gentlemen. Let us eat in the Gagarin manner". She picked up her biggest spoon too. Later, in a moment of candour, she told Yuri Gagarin: "I don't know how to use them myself. The servants hand me the right one". (11)

But do you know what happened to me? Buckingham Palace, a breakfast meeting with the English queen. Ancient protocol, very strict. Very,

very few people are honoured with breakfast with the queen. Two people at the table, the Queen and me – her guest: to the left and the right of me, a staggering number of items to be used, depending on the dish that's served. I say with a smile: "Your Majesty, this is the first time I've had breakfast with Her Majesty the Queen, I'm a simple man, only yesterday I was just a flying officer, forgive me if I unwittingly offend against etiquette". The Queen replies, smiling: "Dear Mr. Gagarin, I was born and grew up in this palace and, believe me, I still don't know in which order to use all these knives and forks". And she adds in a whisper: "Every time, take the knife and fork that are on the outside". (16)

Gagarin, having finished his tea, fished the slice of lemon out of his cup and ate it – to the horror of all present: however, the well-mannered queen immediately followed his example, swallowing her own slice and saying with a smile: "Delicious!" (61)

Mikhail Veller, *Samovar*
Gagarin gobbled up the lemon from his cup when he was having tea with the Queen of England and she aristocratically defused the awkwardness by doing the same and since that precedent, etiquette allows the lemon from the cup to be eaten. (22)

Vladimir Lebedev, Supervisor of Cosmonauts' Medical and Psychological Training at Zvezdny Gorodok
Later Gagarin told us the following story. As a village lad, all he knew about kings and queens came from fairytales. But now, after the official reception, the Queen had invited him to lunch. Yura told us he wanted so badly to make certain she was a real live queen, that he touched her under the table, just above the knee. She smiled and carried on drinking her coffee. At the time, Lyosha Leonov exclaimed: "Yura, you're kidding!" Gagarin didn't try to prove anything. When I started writing my memoirs, I recalled this story and I wanted to check if Yura was joking. In the English newspapers that covered his visit, they wrote that the queen expressed her admiration

for Gagarin's heroism and even violated the provisions of protocol. She walked up to the cosmonaut in delight and started squeezing him with her hands. And apart from that, the queen was photographed with Gagarin, which his status did not permit, because he was a commoner. But the queen got out of that situation by saying that Gagarin, having flown into space, was a man of the sky. (56)

Quebec Chronicle-Telegraph
With women, Gagarin has the traditional shy formality of the Russian. (45)

The Queen gave her wide smile. The interview was over. How the Queen conveyed the information had always been a mystery to Sir Claude, but it was as plain as if a bell had rung. (2)

"And how do you like our Gagarin, My Lady?" "Oh, he is quite charming ... I read in the newspapers that almost all our young London girls have already fallen in love with him ... And it's no wonder. By the way, how old is he?"
"Twenty-seven."
"What a pity that I am not as young as that brave person who gave Gagarin a kiss outside your embassy yesterday."
"What do you mean, My Lady?" one of us said, clumsily trying to pay her a compliment. "Looking at you, you could be the same age as our hero."
"Thank you. I had no idea that Russians could be so sweet." (9)

... suddenly he held out his diary: "Look through that! It might come in handy. Meanwhile I'll sort out the post!" The first thing to catch my eye was this entry, written in an almost calligraphic hand: "Had breakfast with the queen at Buckingham Palace. How about that! The Queen received me well. She was amiable and correct. I gave her the book The Road to Space ... She was really pleased ..." (59)

Headline in *The Daily Mail*: MAKE HIM SIR YURI! (44)

Khwaja Ahmad Abbas, *Till We Reach the Stars*

Yuri's London visit was, of course, very important for Anglo-Soviet relations, as for the first time so many Englishmen were able to see an ordinary Soviet young man who was not a politician or an ideologue and yet who had become a representative of his people. But no less important was the impact of this visit on Soviet people themselves. For the three days he was away, his visit to England was the subject of much animated conversation in Moscow. [...] After all, apart from diplomatic visits by the leaders of the Government, it was for the first time that an ordinary Soviet man had gone among the capitalists, the aristocrats and the 'gentlemen' (the English word is used in the Russian language too) of England, to meet them as equals and to be honoured by them for this remarkable feat which was no less the proud achievement of his whole people. They were as happy about the generous and enthusiastic welcome that all sections of the British public gave him as they were gratified that their young man had held his own in those alien surroundings and had come out with flying colours. "Now they will know," a young Moscow journalist told me, looking at pictures of Yuri's London reception in *The Daily Worker*, "what we ordinary Soviet people are like."(1)

From the palace, Gagarin went to the Soviet Trade Fair and made a surprise speech to 5000 British boys and girls attending the fair.
"I hope many of you here in this hall will be able to make space flights, perhaps as passengers, pilots, scientists on space missions, perhaps in another capacity, but most of all as passengers".
"Space flying requires a certain amount of sound knowledge in the sciences, in mathematics and other subjects. I would like to wish you every happiness in your life, a good time, lots of fun and in general – everything of the best".
He was enthusiastically cheered. (39)

When the programme of meetings, trips and press conferences had been exhausted, we devoted several hours to a visit to Highgate Cemetery, the resting place of the remains of the founder of scientific communism, Karl Marx. The road there runs through workers' districts and although this trip was not listed in our plans, the working people of London realised that a Soviet cosmonaut could not fly out of the British capital without having visited the grave of Karl Marx. That is why on that day all the streets adjoining Highgate Cemetery were crowded with construction workers, dockers, metalworkers, electricians and railway workers ... (10)

St Petersburg Times
A crowd of 3,000 watched as Gagarin placed the wreath of red and white roses [on Marx's grave] and saluted. He then stood stiffly at attention for two minutes in pouring rain before returning to his car. (37)

I was at school in Highgate in North London. Karl Marx's grave was in Highgate cemetery, where every Russian dignitary had to come and pay their respects. We were given the afternoon off school: now most of my friends went off to play cricket or football, play with their Game Boys or whatever it was one did in 1961. But for some reason I decided to go to Highgate cemetery and see what was going on. [...] I was bowled over by the experience: this man – who was very small, much smaller than I expected, he seemed to be dwarfed by this big army hat he was wearing – he'd been in space for 93 minutes and I couldn't believe it. And that was the moment for me, I wanted to do something in space. I didn't know what, but I wanted to have a part of it. (50)

Everywhere he went during his five-day stay, cheering crowds swarmed about him. Yuri invariably handled them with all the charm and poise of a professional diplomat (unlike Britain's protocol department, which was put into such a blue funk by Yuri's uninvited, unofficial visit that it sent only a minor civil servant to the airport to greet him). (44)

In reflecting these aspirations, Gagarin struck a chord with a workforce who lived under the constant threat of thermo-nuclear war and attempted to capture something of the spirit of Khrushchev's new, more open and vibrant U.S.S.R. That the dreams of rapprochement and socialist advance, cherished by the Soviet premier and his protégé, were ultimately to evaporate amidst Kennedy's blockade of Cuba and a return to the arms race, was by no means clear in the summer of 1961. The subtle manner in which Gagarin's visit to Britain had been handled - as opposed to the heavy handed treatment afforded to his later and quite disastrous mission to Gomulka's Poland - ensured that the reputation of the U.S.S.R. probably stood higher with the British public at that moment than at any point since May 1945, while the order books of the Soviet firms who exhibited at Earls Court were filled in record time by their anxious commercial rivals. (48)

Khrushchev had scored a valuable public relations success in the West, while for Gagarin himself, the visit had been nothing short of a triumph: confirming his diplomatic skills and conferring upon him a political role which had not yet become onerous. Yet perhaps the most durable effect of his visit to these shores and the one which Gagarin would probably have been best pleased with, was the sense of idealism and hope which he had inspired in the hearts and minds of British working people. This, at least, was enough to transcend the harsh realities of the Cold War era and to signal a better way ahead. (48)

By week's end the spaceman's boyish smile and unfailing modesty had conquered all Britain. (44)

Against the background of the Berlin crisis, the escalating conflict in Vietnam and the abortive American invasion of Cuba, this spontaneous outpouring of popular sentiment in honour of a Soviet airman, acting as an unofficial ambassador, may at first sight appear incongruous. However, upon closer inspection the reasons behind the genuine warmth of Gagarin's reception are not hard to discern. In marked contrast to the ageing Soviet leadership, Yuri was young, dynamic and glamorous. Possessing an unaffected charm and an outgoing personality, his fame rested securely on his own bravery, skill and athleticism. As a result, he appealed equally to both men and women, the young and the old. (48)

The 27-year old air force major was besieged by a screaming mob of 2,000 when he left the Soviet embassy in London to drive to the airport. Women fought to get near his open limousine. Several fell to the ground screaming. Shrubs and bushes were trampled and the embassy's lawn was torn up. But as always, Gagarin remained calm and imperturbable, smiling, waving and raising his cap to the crowd. (40)

Gagarin stood up in an open grey Rolls-Royce en route to the airport, waving and smiling as the crowds in the streets recognized and cheered him (41)

As his TU-104 airliner took off for home, the cheers of thousands on the roof of the airport building could be heard above the roar of the jet engines.
While he was climbing the steps of the plane, mechanics and others rushed forward to shake his hand, pat him on the back and embrace him.
His departure was a dramatic climax to one of the most enthusiastic receptions ever accorded to a foreign personality in Britain. (40)

During Yuri Alexeevich Gagarin's stay, English propaganda already made efforts to impress on English people that they should not identify Yuri Alexeevich Gagarin's "personal merits" with the politics of the USSR. (63)

Back in Moscow, Nikita Khrushchev, musing on Yuri's triumph, may well have decided that Gagarin's first flight into space would be his last: Public Relations Master Yuri was obviously too hot a talent to waste in space. (44)

Soviet Astronaut Yuri Gagarin is the newest figure in the Tussaud waxworks. A model of Maj. Gagarin will go on display next month, close to the figure of Soviet Premier Khrushchev. (46)

Quebec Chronicle-Telegraph
He has brought a breath of personal daring back into an age dominated by machines. Somehow this, coming from a nation thought of as more dehumanized than most, is especially endearing. (45)

REFERENCES

English Books (Alphabetically by author)
Khwaja Ahmad Abbas, *Till We Reach the Stars: The Story of Yuri Gagarin*, Asia Publishing House, London, 1961
Alan Bennett, *The Uncommon Reader*, Second Edition, Faber and Faber, London, 2007 (pp. 41-2, 99)
Rebel Journalism. The Writings of Wilfred Burchett, edited by George Burchett. Cambridge University Press, 2007
Lewis Carroll, *Alice in Wonderland*
Jonathan Coe, *What a Carve-Up*, Viking, London, 1994, pp.19-20
Tom Wolfe, *The Right Stuff*, Jonathan Cape, London, 1979, p. 239

Russian Books (Alphabetically by author)
The Soviet Space Initiative in State Documents, 1946-1964 (Sovietskaia kosmicheskaia initsiativa v gosudarstvennikh dokymentakh, 1946-1964), edited by Yu.M. Baturin, Moscow, 2010
S. Borzenko, N. Denisov, *The First Cosmonaut (Pervyi kosmonavt)*, Moscow, 1969
N. N. Denisov, *Good, Good, Gagarin! (Khorosho, khorosho, Gagarin!)*, Moskovskii rabochii, Moscow, 1963
N.N. Denisov, *Straight to the Issue: Recollections of a War Correspondent (Srochno v nomer: vospominaniia voennogo zhurnalista)*, Voenizdat, Moscow, 1978
Extracts from the personal diary of Yuri Gagarin, quoted in: V. Gagarina, *108 Minutes and a Whole Life, (108 minut i vsya zhizn')*, Second Edition, Molodaia gvardiia, Moscow, 1982
Klaus Gestwa, "Gagarin, the Columbus of Space. The culture of memory and the cult of heroes in comparative perspective", in *The Trajectory into Today: A deposit of historical and biographical artefacts (Traektoriia v segodnia: rossyp' istoriko-biograficheskikh artefaktov)*, edited by O.S Nagornaia, O.Iu. Nikonova, Iu.Iu. Khmelevskaia. "Encyclopedia", Chelyabinsk, 2009
N.P. Kamanin, *The Concealed Cosmos (Skrytyi kosmos)*, Infortext, Moscow, 1995-1997
N. P. Kamanin, 'Ready. I'm determined!' ("Gotov. Reshaius'!) in *Iu. A. Gagarin (on the 50th anniversary of his birth) - (Iu. A. Gagarin (K 50-letiiu so dnia rozhdeniia)*, Znanie, Moscow, 1984
N.P. Kamanin, Fliers and Cosmonauts (Letchiki i kosmonavty), Politizdat, Moscow, 197
A.I. Kamshalov, in Yuri Ustinov (ed.), *Gagarin's Immortality (Bessmertie Gagarina)*, Geroi otechestva, Moscow, 2004
Oleg Kudenko, *The Orbit of Life (Orbita zhizni)*, Moskovskii rabochii, Moscow, 1971
N. Nosov, *Dunno on the Moon (Neznaika na Lune)*, Moscow, 1964
V.I. Rossoshansky, *The Gagarin Phenomenon (Fenomen Gagarina)*, Saratov State Economic University, Saratov, 2001
Son of the Earth: A Book about the Saratov Years in the Life of Y.A. Gagarin (Syn zemli: kniga o saratovskikh godakh zhizni Iu.A.Gagarina), Privolzhskaia, Saratov, 1985
Mikhail Veller, *Samovar*, Miry, Jerusalem, 1996 (21)
Maria Zaliubovskaia, *Son of Earth and the Stars. A Lyrical Story about Gagarin (Syn zemli i zvezd, Liricheskaya povest' o Gagarine)*. TsK LKSMU Press "Molod", Kiev, 1980.

English Articles (chronologically)

The Ottawa Citizen, 11 July 1961
The Glasgow Herald, 12 July 1961
The Miami News, 12 July 1961
The Palm Beach Post, 12 July 1961
The Times, 12 July 1961
The Southeast Missourian, 12 July 1961
The Daily Express, 13 July 1961, p. 3
The Ottawa Citizen, 13 July 1961
The Glasgow Herald, 13 July 1961
The Age, 13 July 1961
The Palm Beach Post, 14 July 1961
The Age, 15 July 1961
The St. Petersburg Times, 15 July 1961
The Straits Times, 15 July 1961, p.2
"Yuri lunches with Queen, honors Marx", The Washington Post, 15 July 1961, p. 15
"Gagarin home after wild British sendoff", The Los Angeles Times, 16 July 1961
"Yuri given big sendoff by Britons", The Washington Post, 16 July 1961, p. 16
"Britain plays foolishly with Communist Fireball", The Herald Journal, 16 July 1961
Flight, 20 July 1961
Time Magazine, 21 July 1961
The Quebec Chronicle-Telegraph, 21 July 1961, p. 10
Edmonton Journal, 31 July 1961
The Ottawa Citizen, 31 July 1961, p. 6
John Callow, 'Yuri Gagarin in Manchester', Working Class Movement Library Bulletin, No. 10, 1990
Richard Thorpe, 'Leadership and Change: Prime Ministers in the Post-War World –Macmillan', Lecture given at Gresham College, 30 November 2005; transcript available at http://www.gresham. ac.uk/event.asp?PageId=45&EventId=445
John Zarnecki, Principal Investigator for the study of surface problems in the Huygens Project, Lecture available at http://www.open2.net/oulecture2007/ yuri.html (12/6/07)
Boris Belitsky, interpreter, 2009: http://english/ruvr. ru/radio_broadcast/2248140/
Francis Spufford, "The Red Plenty: lessons from the Soviet dream", Guardian, Review,7 August 2010

Russian Articles (Chronologically)

N.P. Kamanin, 'A Citizen of the Soviet Union', *Aviation and Cosmonautics*, ('Grazhdanin sovietskogo soiuza', *Aviatsiia i kosmonavtika*), No.1, 1962, pp. 70-77
Alexander Soldatov, Ambassador of the USSR to Great Britain in 1961; a document dated 9 March, 1990
Kommersant, 27 March 1998
'Why was Gagarin Smiling?' ('Pochemu Gagarin ulybalsia?', *Moskovskii komsomolets*, 13-20 April 2000
Cited in V. Gubarev, 'Her Mighty Menacing Majesty' ('Ee Velichestvo kuz'kina mat'), *Parlamentskaia gazeta*, 3 November 2004
Rabochii put', 2 August 2007
Izvestiya, 28 October 2008
http://interwiki.info/index.php?title=□□□□□□ (4 June 2009)
Evgenii Kliuev, 'A Slice of Lemon as a Sign of Culture' ('Lomtik limona kak priznak kul'tury') http://www.tverlife.ru/news/19300.html (26 March 2010)
Georgii Mitasov, 'Sometimes "Zhiguli" won at billiards', *Ogoniok*: www.ogoniok.com/ archive/2004/4839/12-62-63/
http://cosmosravelin.narod.ru/r-space
Interview with Jonathan Coe, afisha.ru

.

ANNA STAROBINETS
THE LIVING ONE
(EXTRACT)

Translated by Andrew Bromfield

Greetings from
"Renaissance"
the Universal Historical Data Bank

Attention!
This unit contains only private letters and documents.

This unit has been leased for 120 years with the option of subsequent extension.

Access to this cell is limited exclusively to the leaseholder.

Access to this cell is not available to the leaseholder
if he has not yet reached the age of eight.

Enter your incode.

Thank you,
incode accepted.

Place your incode holder's electronic plastic card
against the glowing area of the screen.

Thank you,
card accepted.
Place your left hand
against the glowing area of the screen.

Identification failed.

Attention!
Make certain that the palm of your hand
Is pressed firmly against the glowing area of the screen
and try again.

Identification failed.

Sorry,
You have been denied access to this cell.

The Universal Historical Data Bank
"Renaissance"
will report this attempt to ...

Attention!
Session aborted
You have entered the POS level 1 access code.

Level 1 access code accepted.

Level 2 access code accepted.

Level 3 access code accepted.

The POS triple code is being processed ...

This unit contains only private letters and documents.

The data bank is not responsible for the accuracy of information contained in this unit.

Attention!
The triple code has been processed.

Triple code accepted.

You may now access the unit as a *visitor*.

Pleasant reading.

There is no death.

PART ONE

Hannah

Document No. 1 (personal recording of the leaseholder)

September of the year 439 b.l.o.
First day of the waning moon

The doctor who did my tests was not too concerned at first. He simply said that the connection was not functioning properly, so he would have to do everything again and sorry for making me wait. He froze, looking past me, right through me, with his eyes not blinking. His pupils contracted and expanded erratically, in a strange, twitchy rhythm. Then a steady rhythm set in and for some reason he closed his eyes. As if he wasn't able to hold three levels – but that never happens with doctors ... So he must have gone deeper. What for? There was a sudden, acrid smell of sweat in the room and I held my breath. I noticed that his eyebrows and forehead and the flaps of this nose, were glittering with moisture. I thought: there's something wrong with him, with this doctor, he's the one who's not functioning properly, the connection's perfectly fine.
When he opened his eyes again, his face looked as if he'd seen the incode of the Butcher's Son – or not even the incode, but Butcher's Son himself, with the weary smile of a diligent worker and a bloody, stinking axe, like in the serial "Eternal Killer".
"I have to perform the procedure again," he said and I noticed that his hands were shaking.

"For the third time?"

He didn't answer, just removed one sensor from my stomach and attached another one exactly the same.

We sat in silence for about a minute: me in the huge, cold chair and him facing me. I thought: if there is someone from the Black List there inside me, some maniac, like the Butcher's Son or the Corrupt One – then I shall never see him, not even once and they'll keep him in a house of correction, in a solitary cell, they'll feed him three times a day and not say a single word to him, he'll never understand what's going on. I thought what hypocrisy it is to call them houses of correction. No one ever tries to correct anything there. A full stomach and complete silence ...

Then the sensor squeaked and the doctor computed the result. It looked me as if it was the same.

I asked:

"Is something wrong?"

He didn't answer.

"Is there something wrong with the child?"

He stood up and walked around the room.

"His father ..." – the doctor's voice trembled like a beer can rolling across concrete. "Do you know him?"

"No. He's a festival child."

"Get dressed. And wait out in the corridor. I'll call a POS officer.".

"Is he abnormal?"

"I beg your pardon?"

"The child. My Kin. Is my Kin from the Black List?"

"Ah ... no ..." he finally looked at me, but in a strange sort of way: as if he was watching me from a distance, through binoculars. As if I was hovering somewhere on the horizon. As if I was in the socium, but not here, with him. No, your Kin is not from the Black List."

"Then why the POS officer? What have I done? What is my transgression?"

"That's outside my competence," he said abstractedly and immediately stopped noticing me anymore. He was obviously involved in some other conversation on a deep level.

The officer was in no great hurry. It took him forty minutes to get there and I spent those forty minutes in the corridor, watching the females going in through the doors of the doctor's rooms, all tense and irritable, all in the usual state of fright at the revelation to come, trying to prepare themselves for the worst, but clinging stubbornly to hope for the best. Hope. They simply radiated hope. Waves of toxic hope flooded the entire corridor. Maybe it will be all right. Maybe not now. Maybe I'm empty.

They come out of the rooms changed. Emptied, walking with the smooth, rapid stride of dancers, they seem to become slimmer, the emptiness swirling inside them seems to make them lighter.

The others tread heavily, as if they have put on weight all of a sudden. Their gaze is turned inward; oh, that well-known gaze of submission – appraising, trying to discern and understand superfluity that is growing there within.

Submission, responsibility, duty – that's what the psycho therapists will tell them tomorrow. Submission to Nature.Responsibility to their Kin.And duty to the Living One. Yes, it's hard. Those three components of harmony are inconvenient. But you will find consolation in the other three. Satisfaction, stability, immortality. And now let's all stand in a circle and hold hands – those who wish can put on contact gloves, they're sterile and let us repeat this together: "The harmony of the Living One consists of six components: submission, duty, responsibility, satisfaction, stability and immortality". And now let us all say together: "The harmony of the Living One depends on me personally".

My psychotherapist believes that tactile contact and speaking in unison is the best possible training. Painful, but useful. He says the round dance and the chorus are a kind of model. In a round dance you realise you are part of the Living One far more clearly than in the socium ... In a round dance, you feel far more protected. In a round dance you are not even frightened of the Five Seconds of Darkness.

"... there is no death!" The planetary officer plonked himself down on the empty chair beside me and put his square black briefcase beside his feet: the mirror mask stuck to his face was a little dull, smeared with something. "It's hot today ..."

"What is my transgression?"

"You have not committed one."

"Then why do you wish to interrogate me?"

"It's my job." The planetary officer glanced at me intently and – as far as I could tell from the expression of the mask – with abhorrence. "Put this on, please."

He handed me another mirror mask, also not very clean

"Do we have to use a tell-tale?"

"The appliance is obligatory for conducting a conversation," he said, impatiently shaking the mask that he was holding out. "Put it on. The inside is quite sterile. Good, thank you, Hannah ... This is simply a conversation. Nothing like an interrogation ..."

The mask was cold. Cold and sticky, like the touch of some deep-sea creature.

"... I will now connect your mask to the device for conducting a conversation ... Aha ... and now mine ... There. This is simply in order to record our conversation, nothing more."

His voice under the mask underwent a sudden, disgusting transformation, changing into a monotonous kind of drone.

"... At the end of the conversation you will receive a verbatim record. The conversational device cannot cause any harm to you or your ... er ... embryo, it is made of environmentally benign ..."

"What is my transgression?"

"You have not committed one."

"I don't understand what's going on."

"Neither do I." He smiled with his mirror mouth. "I don't understand either. That's why I need you to tell me everything about your ... er, er ... embryo, in as much detail as possible."

"It's a festival child."

"I said in detail ..."

Do you wish to discontinue working with document No. 1?

yes   *no*

Work with this document has been discontinued

Change *to another document or discontinue work with this unit?*

Changing to document No. 3 ...

Document No. 3 (copy of verbatim report of conversation with POS officer on 10.09.439 b.l.o.)

POS officer: You are required to tell me everything about your embryo, in as much detail as possible.

Interviewee 3678: It's a festival child.

POS officer: I said in detail.

Interviewee 3678: Today, the first day of the waning moon, I came to Medical Centre No. 1015 in compliance with the law on the monthly verification of the size of the population. The doctors determined that I was pregnant ...

POS officer: Had you previously visited the Centre regularly?
Interviewee 3678: Yes, of course. I come here every month.

POS officer: Had the doctors at the Centre ever previously determined that you were pregnant?

Interviewee 3678: No. It was the first time it had happened.

POS officer: Did you not have any previous sexual contacts?

Interviewee 3678: Yes, I did.

POS officer: Did you have fertility problems?

Interviewee 3678: No.

POS officer: Then why was this the first pregnancy?

Interviewee 3678: I used contraceptives.

POS officer: That is forbidden.

Interviewee 3678: I have permission.

Interviewee 3678 rummages in her handbag. The sensor records an increase of 0.3 degrees in body temperature, an increase in pulse rate to 130 a minute, a dilation of the pupil to 6.3 mm., which exceeds the norm for the ambient light intensity.

Interviewee 3678: There.

Interviewee 3678 shows the POS officer a document, a permit to use contraceptives, issued on the basis of a medical diagnosis of mild psychological abnormality.

POS officer: Tell me about the festival in more detail.

Interviewee 3678: The child was conceived at the Regional Festival for the Support of Nature at the last new moon, within the terms of the programme for population control and in accordance with the law on planned ...

POS officer: Would you recognise the father?

Interviewee 3678: Are you joking?

POS officer: I'm just doing my job.

Interviewee 3678: How could I recognise the father? I told you, the child was conceived at a festival. How could I know which of them ...
POS officer: How many partners did you have at the festival?

Interviewee 3678: Five ... Seven ... I don't know,

POS officer: According to ourinformation, at that Festival for the Support of Nature, three thousand, three hundred and two men visited the Reproduction Zone. We will present all of them to you for identification. Will you be able to identify your partners among them?

Interviewee 3678: I don't know. I'm not sure ... I'm not obliged to do that. The law on the privacy of sexual relations is still in force.

POS officer: Naturally, you are not obliged to do this. It is only a request. A request from the Planetary Order Service.

Interviewee 3678: I will do as you request, if you explain to me what is going on here.

POS officer: Very well, I will try to explain to you. In the Pause Zone at the Festival for the Support of Nature in which you participated, the existence of six hundred and ten people was temporarily terminated. At the same time six hundred and eleven people were conceived in the Reproduction Zone. Six hundred and ten of them are direct reincarnations of those who remained in the Pause Zone, all the incodes correspond precisely. And only one – your festival child ...

Interviewee 3678: And you frightened me so badly just for that! Weebep![1] [1. A popular abbreviation used in socium chats: "I weep before the pause". Incorporated into first-level lexis from the second century b.l.o.]
That's really absurd. It has been proved that in 95 per cent of cases festival children reproduce the pausers in a stable fashion, but in the remaining cases the incodes could be absolutely anybody's. Did you stick this thing on my face just to tell me that my Kin's incode doesn't match any of the pausers? So what, I couldn't care less whose incode

the child has, sweterin[2] [2. A popular acronym in socium chats: "I swear on the eternal incode". Incorporated into first-level lexis from the third century b.l.o.] as long as it's not some criminal's ... He isn't a criminal, is he?

POS officer: I don't know.

Interviewee 3678: But I do. The doctor said my Kin isn't from the Black List.

POS officer: That is correct. Your embryo's incode is not among the incodes on the Black List.

Interviewee 3678: Then what's the problem?

POS officer: The problem is that the incode of your embryo ... the incode of your Kin isn't listed anywhere at all.

Interviewee 3678: I don't understand. That doesn't make sense!

POS officer: But it's true. His incode is not the same as any of the incarnation codes in the global data base: not one of the three billion. In effect, your future child doesn't have any incode at all. Instead of an incode, the result from both devices used for your intrauterine inspection was nil.

Interviewee 3678: Nil?

POS officer: Nil, zero. He has no in-history. Your Kin has never lived before.

Interviewee 3678: You mean ... but ... in that case ... whose place has he taken? Does that mean someone who temporarily ceased to exist was not reproduced? He disappeared? Is that it?

POS officer: Not at all. No one has disappeared. A new person has been added.

Interviewee 3678: That's impossible! You're a Planetary Order Service officer, aren't you ashamed of yourself? Are you a member of some kind of sect? This is heresy you're speaking. It is said: "The number of the Living is invariable. The Living One is three billion lives and not one shall be taken away from it and not one shall be added, for in eternal reproduction there lies ..."

POS officer: You needn't bother, I have also read the Book of Life and learned the key passages off by heart. But a fact is a fact. The quantitative composition of the Living One has changed and it is now three billion and one. And the one is your Kin, with his zero incode. I'm afraid you don't realise just how serious this is. Nobody does yet

Interviewee 3678: Could he ... could my Kin be dangerous to the harmony of the Living One?

POS officer: It's not out of the question.

Interviewee 3678: Will they put him in a house of correction? Why are you shaking your head? He ... will they not let him be born? Will I have to have an abortion?

POS officer: I don't decide matters like that. Over the next seven days the "zero problem" will be considered at the very highest level. And for those seven days you will stay in the clinic, under the supervision of the doctors. You have no right to leave your ward until the Council of Eight delivers its judgement. Tomorrow the first three hundred men who took part in the festival will be brought to you for identification. Is that all clear?

Interlocutrix 3678: Yes

POS officer: I have one last question for you. If you have permission to use contraceptives, which did you not take precautions at the festival?

Interviewee 3678: Because I wanted to conceive a child.

POS Officer: In what sense?

Interviewee 3678: In the simplest possible. I wanted a child.

POS officer: Explain your thought to me.

Interviewee 3678: The medical certificate allows me to use contraceptives, but it doesn't release me from my supreme duty to the Living One. I was performing my duty. Is there something about that you don't like?

POS officer: Well, of course not. Your attitude is worthy of every respect. Thank you for this conversation.

(end of verbatim record)

<u>Change</u> to another document or <u>discontinue</u> work with this unit?

cerberus: How about a beer?

Attention! You should now <u>change</u>to another document or<u>discontinue</u> work with this unit.

"That's enough, Ef, finish it. Let's have a beer. This data bank's so stuffy. It's like being up the Living One's backside. And this damn mask will melt on my face if I don't get a swallow of something cool soon!"

<u>Change</u> to another document or <u>discontinue</u> work with this cell?

"Okay, you've persuaded me," said Ef, jabbing sluggishly at "discontinue" with his bandaged hand.

The faceless one

There's no one about. It isn't dark yet, but the golden glow from the little lamps set in between the slabs of the pavement is already illuminating the evening mist and the tender-pink, white-veined marble.

Cleo: there is no death, Ef, if you are here

Ef's shoes leave black tracks of soot on the marble and the electronic cleaning woman standing motionless by the payment in a bikini and rubber gloves switches on with a quiet click, goes down on her hands and knees and starts wiping it off. She crawls after them quickly, pivoting her backside provocatively and moaning in a low monotone. Naturally, her kind has to provoke the desire to breed and propagate in people passing by.

Cerberus turns back and spits a thick gobbet onto the pink marble. The cleaning woman meekly reaches for the gobbet with her rag.

"Bugger off!" Cerberus laughs and prods her gently in the face with his pointed shoe. The cleaning woman stops and, without opening her plastic lips, moans sensually: "wow".

cerberus: *there's a good bar round the corner*

cerberus: *do you hear what I'm saying?*

cerberus: *ef!*

"There's a good bar on the corner of Harmony Boulevard," Cerberus says out loud. "What is it, are you offline?"

ef: *no sorry just lost in thought. ok. let's go to harmony.*

They turn to the left. Harmony Boulevard is empty: the concrete sculpture of a huge bronze-coloured hand looks lonely, as if it waiting desperately for a handshake from someone ... there is only the halfwit Matthew, a tall, skinny old man, wandering round the base of the concrete mass, shaking his little bell and shouting insistently:

"He died for us! He died for our sins! He died for us!"

cleo: is everything all right?

"Committing a violation, are we?" Cerberus snarls. "Using those words?"

"Oh, he is the beginning and the end!" Matthew howls. "His name is Zero! He died for us! He burned in the sacred fire!"

cleo: *I get worried when you're grey for so long* J

" ... he died, he died for us!"

"Shut up!" Ef snarls. It's lucky for you lucky that I want a beer. Or I'd have you down at the house of correction like a shot!"

"Oh, you bloody hounds of hell! Myrmidons of the devil! Men with mirror faces! Men without faces! Tremble, for he cometh. And the kingdom shall be his. And his will shall rule! For you are devils. And you shall be cast down! You shall be overthrown! For he died for us! For he is the Saviour! And his name is Zero!"

cleo: *maybe your connection's not working? I'll contact the support service*

The beer tastes of iron. Maybe it's the beer, or maybe it's the mask clinging to his nose

and lips that gives the beverage the metallic taste. Ef runs his tongue over the inside of his cheek. No, it's not the mask. His cheek has split against his teeth, it's bleeding, that's all.

Cerberus come back with a second mug of beer, slumps heavily into the opposite chair, immediately sucks in a third of the mug and fixes the stare of the soft, vacant ovals of his mirror eyes on Ef again. Those eyes reflect Ef's eyes, in which those eyes are reflected and they reflect ... Ef starts feeling sick, as if he's in a boat pitching and rolling on the sea, he lowers his head and looks into his mug. The foamy surface of the beer doesn't reflect anything.

cerberus: *was there anything he said, that zero, before he ...* Cerberus looks round at the empty tables and, just to be on the safe side, he moves closer ... *before he ... you know ... destroyed himself*

ef: *listen, I just want to be like everyone else.***cerberus**: *what's that you want ef?*

ef: *me? I want to sleep, but before he died that zero said: listen, I just want to be like everyone else.*

cerberus: *don't say that!*

"Don't say that, Ef!" Cerberus was clearly feeling nervous. He was so nervous that even the steady drone into which the mask transformed his voice sounded a tone higher. "Don't talk about death. There is no death." Cerberus nodded significantly at the telltale under the table and twirled one finger beside his temple. As if to say: It all gets recorded, you idiot.

STP_19: *connection problems? our support service adjusts your connection quickly and efficiently at any time of the day or night. personal contact is not necessary!*

"There was death for him," Ef said wearily. "For Zero. You know he was born without an incode. And yesterday he died. Exploded a wonder-sun and died. There aren't any more Zeros, Cerberus. He has no continuation — all the population control centres confirm that. It's not a pause. It's death."

cerberus: *there's just one thing I don't understand. how could he CRUSH a wonder-sun in his HAND? that takes more than human strength ... maybe he wasn't human at all?*

ef: *according to all the biological data he was human. I think he must just have fiddled with it beforehand, unscrewed something maybe ... or else it was faulty which happens sometimes too.*

cerberus: *ok in any case it's for the best anyway, for the Living One.* Cerberus stretches his mirror lips that are wet with beer into a smile and drones flatly: "The number of the Living is invariable, the Living One is three billion live units and not one shall be taken away and not one shall be added. And no more zeros. Are you glad?"

"I am," says Ef. "Very glad. Only I'm terribly tired. And my hands hurt." He stirred his bandaged fingers feebly.

"Got badly burned, eh?"

"All the skin came away."

cerberus: *weebep ... what about your face?*

ef: *no not the face I was wearing the mask it's fireproof.*

cerberus: *show me.*

ef: *show you what?*

"Well, your face. You keep touching your cheek. Maybe you burned it after all. Take off the mask and I'll have a look."

Ef jumps up off his chair. And then sits down again.

"Officer Cerberus. You have just suggested that I violate the regulations of the

Planetary Order Service. Your words have been recorded by my device for conducting conversations and therefore I duly ...

POS-service: *third-level access: signal processing: do you wish to make an official complaint?*

ef: *not yet*

"Ok, ok. Stop jumping about like a flea. Just a little check. A joke!" Cerberus droned reassuringly.

"A joke or a check?!"

cerberus: gopoz![1] [1. A popular acronym in socium chats: "go to the pause zone". Used as an insult, in friendly speech it can be used as a joke. Incorporated into first-level lexis from the first century b.l.o. shortly after the first Festival for the Support of Nature was held.] a friendly joke of course.!

Ef looks at his own reflection in Cerberus's mirror features and feels another surge of nausea. He takes a sip of beer. Closes his eyes. It gets worse.

The darkness doesn't come, what appears instead of the darkness is a *structure*, as if he has stuck his face into a flabby termite mound ... Hundreds of little oval cells, a porous, flexible mass. Most of the cells give off a glow of accessible occupancy and pulsate slightly. The others, dull-grey and motionless, seem derelict. Cerberus's cell is also pretending to be uninhabited ...

cerberus: *stop that you've known me forever!*Missing comma / extra space between "that" and "you've"?

ef: *okay forget it*

cleo: *ef!*

One of the accessible cells swells up and expands, as if it is turning into a greedy mouth.

cleo: *ef I know you're there*

He opens his eyes. Cerberus's mirror mask reflects his mirror mask, reflecting Cerberus's mask ... His lower jaw cramps and his tongue as well. He jumps to his feet.

"What's up?"

"I'm going to puke."

autodoctor: *relax. take a deep breath – brea-ea-ea-the out. breathe in – brea-ea-ea-the out. you are overtired. you need to sleep. alcohol is not recommended. more liquids and a walk in the fresh air.*

"Feeling any better?" asks Cerberus, concerned. "Maybe more beer?"

"I'm overtired," says Ef. "I need to sleep. Alcohol is not recommended. A walk in the fresh air is recommended ... There is no death!"

He walks towards the door.

"There is no death," Cerberus responds and belches precisely, covering his mirror-lips with his hand. The "telltale" converts his belch into a brief, desperate howl.

_____

subject: letter of happiness

from: nonconformist

You have a stupid job and before the pause you had a stupid job and after the pause you'll have a stupid job. But you want to be a scriptwriter or a designer. Follow Zero – he came to change your life

!caution! this message could be spam

mark this message as spam?   **yes**   no

Ef marks it as spam, although it's pointless: the "letter of happiness" has already been sent from his address to a dozen friends. It's impossible to stop the process. He ought to know.

Immediately another message:

subject: important

from: dissident well-wisher

Do not be deceived. Leo-Lot's bright beam can shine in both directions, forward and backward ...

Ef reads the message all the way through and feels another layer appearing between his face and the mask – a cold film of sweat. He marks the letter as spam, although he knows that it isn't spam; then he deletes it; he will remember the text verbatim. His heart is beating in the tips of his fingers, his ears and just below his Adam's apple, as if it has exploded into a hundred dwarf hearts and the blood has carried them throughout his body.

perhaps you are feeling afraid? the autodoctor enquires.

Perhaps. But that's none of your business.

When Ef turns onto Harmony Boulevard it starts to rain – suddenly, without any warning splashes, as if an automatic disinfection shower has been switched on at full power. The damp turns the pale-pink marble the colour of raw liver. In the light of the lamps built into the pavement, the drops of rain look like swarms of golden insects drawn to the smell of blood.

cleo: *the support service checked the connection you're just invisible*

The drops of rain tickle the plastic bodies of the electronic cleaning ladies and the cleaning ladies moan obediently. The drops of rain strike gently against Ef's mirror mask, bringing no relief. Bringing no freshness. If he could take it off. If he could take it off and feel the cold moisture ...

"Tremble, for he cometh ... Tremble for he cometh ... Tremble, for he cometh ..." long, lanky Matthew chants, tramping his bare feet up and down on the lamp that he is standing on, in the golden pillar of light. The golden light gleams on his face, his grey curls and his neck.

"Men with no voice!" he declares, livening up at the sight of Ef. "Men with mirror faces!"

Ef slows down.

"There is no death, Matthew. You're wet through. Go home."

He tries to make the words sound gentle, but the telltale chews them up and spits them out as an order.

Matthew opens his cloudy-blue eyes wide and breaks into a trill of squeaky laughter, baring his long, rotten teeth, like a horse's. Then he whines and squats down on his haunches. He traces his bony finger across the bright, wet marble:

"Do you see what colour the ground *really* is? Do you see what colour it really is?"

"Go home," Ef repeats. Then he switches off the telltale and adds: "I see".

cleo: *why do you say that?*

"You have voices inside you," Matthew whispers and his gaze clears for a moment.

"Voices that aren't yours, right?"

"Yes. Of course."

"They're demons!" Matthew clasps his knees in his arms and sways from side to side.

"They're demons. Switch them off. The demons. Switch them off. The demons. Switch them off ..."

————

deactivate connection

do you really want to deactivate the connection with the socium?

yes   no

confirm:

ef: *yes*

attention: in deactivated mode you cannot see the list of your contacts in the socium, communicate within the socium, receive information from the socium and exchange information with other members of the socium. Deactivate connection?

yes   no

attention: in deactivated mode you will not be an active part of the socium. Deactivate connection?

yes   no

"Yes."

You are no longer in the socium.

Do not be concerned, you can restore your connection with the socium at any moment. Attention: it is not recommended to interrupt connection with the socium for more than 30 minutes. If you do not restore the connection yourself, compulsory connection to the socium will occur after 40 minutes.

Zero

... I just want to be like everyone else. I don't want to take too much on myself. I want to be like everyone else. If not now, then later. After the Pause.

Hey you! Hey, you there in the future! I hope you really will exist. I hope you will be me. I hope I shall exist. If you are my continuation, if I am you, forgive me for this stupid incode you have inherited from me ... It has ruined my life – but I really hope that you will manage somehow. That I will manage somehow, there in the future. In about eight years' time ... You are eight, aren't you?

I suppose this is cowardice. It's running away. It's dishonest. But if you do exist, if you are real, then forgive me for what I'm going to do soon. Forgive me if I have ruined your (or should I write "my") mood. Forgive me if I have caused problems for you (ha-ha, for me!) I want you to understand me. I am going to kill myself – yes, yes, forgive me, forgive me again, it's not permitted to say that, I have to say it differently. I am going to "terminate my existence temporarily", "make a pause", but I'm not a fool, after all, I know: for all of them it's a pause, but for me it will simply be a full stop. And so if you do exist, if you will be, then glolop [1] [1. A popular acronym in socium chats: "Glory to the Living One and his particles". Incorporated into first-level lexis from the late second century b.l.o.] it's our victory, it means that we are like everyone else. I am like everyone else. I am a particle of the Living One.

But if you will not be, if you simply don't exist, if I don't exist anymore – if I disappear, die forever, as people used to do earlier, before the Living One was born ... Well, then I am a mistake of nature. A genetic error. An illness. A boil on the body of the Living One. And then things will be better without me. More correct. Simpler. In short, no matter how things end, it will still be better than it is now ...

I always wanted to be like everyone else. But they made me a god. They made me a devil. They made me a fly in a laboratory. They made me very dangerous. They didn't know what they made me.

They drove me into a corner. They left me completely alone.

He will come again today. Ef, the man in the mask. To look for defects, ask mean little questions, rummage around in my insides like a heap of things that belong to no one.

And then I shall burn myself. Let them all see how the wonder-sun burns!

I'm sure you want to understand. If you are me, of course you'll want to understand ... after all, I wanted to very much.

I shall write everything that I know for you. Because you need it.

Because I need to know. I shall need to know everything.

My mother was called Hannah. I shan't write that she is no longer alive, because it's not possible to say that. Because, of course, she does exist. She is continuing her life ... I shall only write that I miss her. I miss her as if she does not exist anymore – ever since she entered the Pause Zone at the Festival for the Support of Nature.

Hannah was her name then. Now she is called Diana and she is fourteen years old. Her eternal name is Miya-31, but I don't like it, it sounds like a brand of washing-machine. She didn't like it either, she always introduced herself as Hannah?. I don't know what name she likes to introduce herself with now. And I don't want to know.

She had very light skin. So light and clear, it was transparent, that's very rare for globaloids.

Her eyes were velvety, like the wings of a chocolate-coloured moth.

When I went to sleep she always sang me a lullaby – that old one about the animals, it's still in the "Children of the Living One" programmes. I think it's installed at the age of three. I'm sure you remember it:

The roe-deer and the ram are sleeping
The sheep and the lizard are sleeping,
The cow, the tiger and elephant are sleeping
And they have a sad dream,
A dream of dark water,
A dream of bitter sorrow,
They dream of a boat with no oarsman
They dream of shadows with no face ...

I was almost nine already, but I always asked for the song. I refused to go to sleep without it. Hannah used to say it wasn't right, that no one sang songs to such big children, that such big children shouldn't live with their mothers at all, they should live in a boarding school and there weren't any lullabies there.

"But I live with you," I used to say.
"Yes, you do," Hannah agreed.
"Then sing."
And she did sing. She had a beautiful voice.

... In the silence the wolves howl.
In his sleep the cat weeps quietly,
The horse snores, the elephant groans.
Dreaming of dark water,
Dreaming of bitter sorrow,
The animals sleep on the cold shore
And the days go flying by ...

"You won't put me in the boarding school, will you?" I used to ask.
"No, I won't," Hannah said.
"And the two of us will always be together?"
"That doesn't happen, my Kinling," Hannah used to say.
She didn't call me by my name – I understood why later: it frightened her, it forced her to gaze into the precipice, into nothing, into the white void with a black ring round it ... She didn't call me Zero. She simply called me Kinling.
"Why?" I whimpered. "Why can't we always be together? We're immortal, aren't we? Let's just agree: when one of us dies ..."
"Kinling!"
"... I meant to say that when one of us temporarily ceases to exist, the other one will simply find him or her and everything will stay the same as before."
"That doesn't happen, Kinling," said Hannah, shaking her head.
That doesn't happen. She was right. I didn't believe she was right until Ef agreed to take me to her.
I wasn't interested at all in the fat little girl that she had turned into. And she wasn't interested in me either.
Nobody needs anyone, my little friend. You don't mind me calling you "little friend", do you? I hope you don't think I'm being too familiar? After all, in the final analysis, I am talking to myself. Or I'm talking to no one at all ...

"Tell me you love me," I used to ask Hannah.
"Don't, Kinling," she would say, suddenly shrinking somehow.
"Why?"
"I've already told you. The Living One is full of love and every particle of him loves every other particle equally. "
"That means you love me, then?"
And she said:
"Yes."
And then she added in a faint voice:
"I love you as I love every particle of the Living One."

"You love me the same way ... the same way as you love crazy Matthew, who shouts as he walks along the street?"
She didn't answer. I was angry.
"Tell me you love me more than anyone else!"
She didn't answer.
"Then sing."
And she did sing.

... On the cold shore
The animals sleep and days fly by,
The days fly by, night comes,
And we cannot help them

On that day when I saw her for the last time, on that day when Hannah went to her final Festival, she said I should go to bed without her. She said she would come back too late. And so she would sing me the song before she left.

The days fly by, night comes,
And we cannot help them
For the cats and the sheep
The end is coming ...
Only you sleep calmly,
My Living One, my little one,
Smiling in your sleep,
Because there is no death.

"There is no death!" she called as she went out
"There is no death!" I answered her.
"I love you," she said. "I love you more than anyone else."

She was thirty-four.
She still had the right to visit the Reproduction Zone at the Festival for the Support of Nature. The reproductive period officially ends at thirty-five.
In another eleven years she would have received messages from the Regional Centre for Population Control with a gentle suggestion that she should visit the Pause Zone. Messages like that start arriving at forty-five.
In another sixteen years she would have received messages from the Regional Centre for Population Control with a harsh recommendation to visit the Pause Zone. Messages like that start to arrive at fifty.
In twenty-six years she could have reached the Compulsory Pause. The measure that is applied to those who have turned sixty and don't want follow the recommendation voluntarily.
For another whole year she had the right to visit the Reproduction Zone at the festival for the Support of Nature.
But she went into the Pause Zone.
She did it because of me. Because they hadn't taken me into the boarding school and had left me with her.Because she sang songs to me.Because she loved me more than anyone else.

BIOGRAPHIES OF WRITERS

THE WRITERS

MIKHAIL SHISHKIN

The author of widely acclaimed novels, Shishkin is admired as a refined stylist whose fiction engages Russian and European literary traditions and forges an equally expansive vision for the future of literature.

Born January 18, 1961 in Moscow, Shishkin worked as a school teacher and journalist. His writing debut in 1993, the short story Calligraphy Lesson, was named Best Debut of the Year by the literary journal Znamya. In 1995 he moved to Switzerland, where he worked as a Russian and German translator within the Immigration Department and specifically with Asylum Seekers. In recent years he has been living both in Moscow and Zurich.

Shishkin's first novel, Larionov's Reminiscences was published in 1994. The two novels which followed earned him the three most prestigious Russian literary awards: The Taking of Izmail (2000) won the Russian Booker Prize and Venus Hair (Maiden's Hair)(2005) was awarded both the National Bestseller Prize and the Big Book prize.

Shishkin's novel Letter-Book (2010) has been greeted with delight by readers and reviewers alike, was acclaimed as the Literary Event of the Year, and came top in the 2010 Imhonet Readers' Prize.

All of his novels have been adapted for Stage Production in Russia.

PAVEL BASINSKY

Pavel Basinsky was born in 1961 in Frolovo, near Volgograd. He studied at Saratov University and at the Maxim Gorky Literary Institute in Moscow. A prolific journalist and author, Basinsky has excelled at a number of genres, from scholarly monographs to experimental novels. Basinsky holds a PhD in Comparative Literature, has sat on the jury of several major Russian literary prizes, such as the Russian Booker, the Alexander Solzhenitsyn Prize and the Yasnaya Polyana Prize, and is the Cultural Editor of Rossiiskaia Gazeta. He is married with two children and lives in Moscow.

Pavel Basinsky's latest book, Leo Tolstoy: Flight from Paradise, came out in July 2010 and within two months had already been reprinted twice. According to sales figures from some of the largest Russian bookshops such as Moskva, Biblioglobus and Moscow House of Books, Escape from Paradise ranks among the top ten most popular books for Summer-Autumn 2010.

EVGENIY VODOLAZKIN

Previously unknown to readers of fiction, Vodolazkin was catapulted to prominence by his debut novel Solovyov and Larionov, which was not only very popular with readers, but was also rewarded with a place on the shortlist for both the Andrei Bely Prize (2009) and the Big Book Award (2010).

Prior to this, Vodolazkin was best known within his academic field of Old Russian literature - a subject on which he is an internationally recognised expert, with degrees from Kiev (the city of his birth), St. Petersburg and Munich universities, and numerous publications to his name. Although he shuns the label 'professorial' for his fiction, Vodolazkin's novel plays with the tools of literary criticism: Solovyov and Larionov are, respectively, a historian and the former White Army General making a life in the Soviet Union (much like Vodolazkin's great-grandfather, to whom the book is dedicated), whose diaries Solovyov researches and analyzes.

Vodolazkin, who is now a regular contributor to newspapers and magazines, is currently working on a novel drawing on his knowledge of Old Russia, which, he promises, will shun the cliches of historical fiction in favour of capturing the spirit and power of the ancient texts that he knows so well.

DINA RUBINA

Dina Rubina is one of the most widely-read Russian authors alive today. She was born in 1953, in Tashkent, Uzbekistan, where she later studied music at the Tashkent Conservatory. At sixteen her first short story appeared in the journal Yunost', which continued to publish her work until the end of the Soviet Union. Life in the colourful environment of Tashkent was not always easy: Rubina had to turn to writing for stage and screen and finally moved to Moscow in the mid-1980s. Rubina's life and adventures since 1990, including her emigration to Israel and her brief return to Russia as a cultural liaison, are reflected in her literary output from that period.

Her most recent novel, On the Sunny Side of the Street, won Russia's Radio Booker Literary Award (2007), the Big Book Literary Prize Bronze Award (2007) and was shortlisted for the Russian Booker (2006). Her latest novels are Leonardo's Handwriting (2008), The White Dove of Cordoba (2009) and The Petrushka Syndrome (2010). Her work has won awards in Uzbekistan, Israel, and France, and has been translated into 20 languages. Her 1996 novel Here Comes the Messiah! is available in English translation, as are several of her shorter pieces.

ALEXANDRA MARININA

Alexandra Marinina (real name - Alexeeva Marina Anatolievna) was born in 1957 in Lvov, Ukraine and until 1971 lived in Leningrad. She moved to Moscow in 1971 and graduated from the Law Faculty of Moscow State University in 1979. She began her service career as a technician and in 1980 she was promoted to Lieutenant of the Militia. She made a study of offenders with mental abnormalities and violent reoffenders. From 1987, she was engaged in analyzing and forecasting crime.

In February 1998, she retired at the rank of Lieutenant Colonel of the Militia. In 1991, she began her literary career with the publication in the journal "Militia" of a detective story entitled "The Six-Winged Seraph", which she co-authored with her colleague A. Gorkin.

In 1992, she started writing a series of detective novels, in which the main character, Anastasia Kamenskaya, is the operations officer of the Moscow Criminal Investigation Department. In addition, she has written numerous prose works, the most significant of which is the family saga *The One Who Knows*, as well as several plays.

In 1995, Marina was awarded the Russian Interior Ministry prize for the best work on the Russian police. In 1998, the Moscow International Book Fair recognized A. Marinina as 'Writer of the Year' and in 2006 she was awarded the 'Writer of the Decade' prize. Her works have been translated and published in more than 25 countries worldwide.

MASTER CHEN (DMITRY KOSYREV)

Dmitry Kosyrev is one of Russia's leading thriller writers. Kosyrev, who writes under the distinctive alias Master Chen, a legacy of his long-standing interest in the Far East, was born in 1955 and studied Chinese history at Moscow State University and the Nanyang University of Singapore.

Since the late 1970s he has been actively involved in the national media, writing on international politics for leading newspapers such as Pravda, Rossiiskaia gazeta and Nezavisimaia gazeta; he is a Member of the Board of the Foreign Policy Association. In addition Kosyrev has been a regular and diverse contributor to many magazines over the last 15 years, writing on wine, food, cigars and travel.

Kosyrev's calling card as a novelist is his intimate knowledge of the Far East: for a long time his home, it provides the settings for his five thrillers novels. His latest thriller – The Pet Foal of the House of Manyakh, set in the 8th century Byzantine Empire – was published at the end of 2010. He is married with two daughters and lives in Moscow.

LEV DANILKIN

Lev Danilkin is the leading literary critic of his generation, credited with making criticism accessible and even glamorous, and is acknowledged, and feared, as the man who can make or break a book. His reviews in the popular cultural digest Afisha are noted for the breadth of their scope and the verve of their writing and are required reading for literate young Russians.

Born in Ukraine in 1974, Danilkin studied at Moscow State University in the early 1990s, at both undergraduate and post-graduate level. He has since worked as the editor-in-chief of Playboy and as the literary critic for the newspaper Vedomosti, as well as for Afisha. In addition to his prodigious journalistic output, Danilkin, a passionate advocate of foreign literature, has translated Julian Barnes's Letters from London and is the author of a pioneering literary biography of the writer and politician Andrei Prokhanov, Man with an Egg, as well as a forthcoming biography of Yuri Gagarin.

ANNA STAROBINETS

Anna Starobinets is one of a handful of Russian authors who writes in the genre of 'intellectual fantasy'.

She was born in Moscow in 1978 and graduated in philology at Moscow State University. As a student she worked part time in several different fields, from simultaneous translation and private tutoring, to billposting and waitressing. After her finishing her degree she started work in journalism. She has worked with the leading Russian newspapers, including Gazeta.ru, Argumenty i Fakty, Expert and Russky reporter, as a reviewer, reporter as well as the culture section editor.

In 2005 Starobinets published her debut collection of mystical short stories Awkward Age and from then on she has been called by critics 'the queen of Russian horror'. This was followed by her first fantasy novel Asylum a year later. Starobinets has written several more collections of short stories, as well as a novella for children, The Land of Good Girls. Her latest novel First Squad: The Truth is based on the Russo-Japanese feature length animation of the same name.

Her anti-utopian fantasy novel The One Who Lives has just come out in Russia, published by AST.

COMPLETE YOUR ROSSICA LIBRARY

Please note that all issues of *Rossica* are priced individually
Please add postage & packing – £2 for the UK and £3 for overseas orders

Red Pyramid
ROSSICA 19: £10
ISBN 978-1-905345-05-2
A literary edition of ROSSICA showcasing the first English translations from nine new works by leading Russian writers.
• Featuring some of Russian fiction's biggest names: Dmitry Bykov, Vladimir Makanin, German Sadulaev and Mikhail Shishkin.
• First appearance in English of extracts of award-winning works such as Makanin's Asan and Slavnikova's 2017.
• Comprehensive introduction by Liza Novikova and exclusive artwork.

The Ties of Blood
ROSSICA 18: £10
ISBN 978-1-905345-04-5
An introduction to some of the gems of contemporary Russian letters, many translated for the first time.
• Short stories from German Sadulaev, Dmitry Novikov and Alexander Ilichevsky.
• Extracts from works by Alexander Ivanov, Dina Rubina and many more.
• Poems by Andrei Rodionov, Alexei Tsvetkov, Maria Galina and more.

Found in Translation
ROSSICA 17: SOLD OUT
ISBN 978-1-905345-03-8
Special issue devoted to the Rossica Translation Prize
• Articles by shortlisted translators
• *The Value and Values of Literary Translation* by Amanda Hopkinson
• Vladimir Nabokov on the translator's craft
• *Pioneers of Russian Translations* by Peter France
• *Borrow in Russia: A Writer in the Making* by John Crowfoot

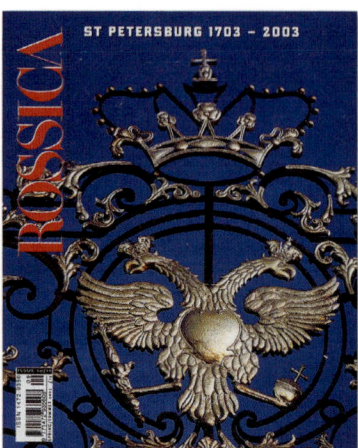

St Petersburg 1703–2003
ROSSICA 10/11: £14
• *Peter the Great and St Petersburg: Between Heaven and Hell* by Lindsey Hughes
• Decoding St Petersburg by Alexander Ivanitsky
• *The Alexander Column: Myth of Empire* by Grigory Sternin
• *Jerusalem on the Neva* by Grigory Kaganov

Redefining Identities in Russian Contemporary Art
ROSSICA 9: £6
From Russian underground art to Post-Soviet experiments
• *Art and Power* by Alexander Borovsky
• *Uniform Pluralism* by Boris Groys
• *The Aesthetics of the Green Square* by Ekaterina Degot
• Exhibitions: Berlin-Moscow; Oleg Prokofiev: Compositions

Dionisy & Kandinsky: Revelations in Colour
ROSSICA 7/8: £14
• *Visions in Colour: Dionisy's Frescoes at the Ferapontov Monastery (16th C.)* by Irina Danilova & Lev Lifshits
• Kandinsky and the Russian Romantic Tradition
• *The Scars Heal. The Colours Come to Life* by Alexander Rappaport
• The History of the Walpole collection

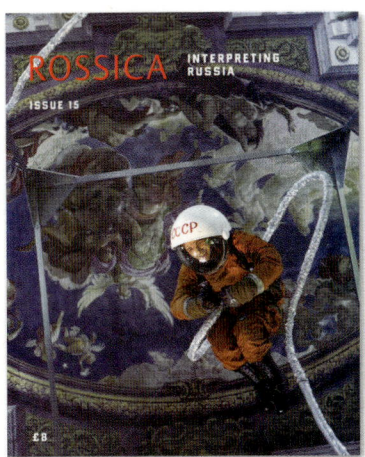

Interpreting Russia
ROSSICA 15: £8
ISBN 978-1-905345-01-4
Special issue devoted to the Rossica
Translation Prize
• Articles by shortlisted translators:
Oliver Ready (Winner), Robert
Chandler, Hugh Aplin, Andrew
Bromfield, Arch Tait, Michael Molnar
• Exhibitions: RUSSIA!, Circling the
Square, The House of Dreams by Ilya
Kabakov

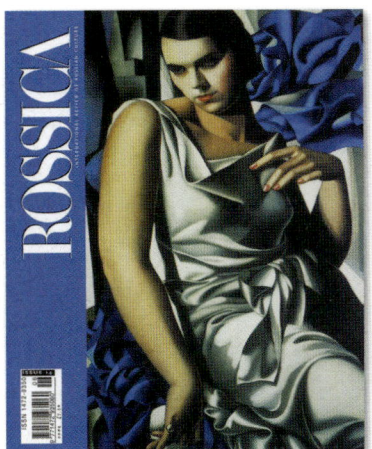

Russian Summer in London
ROSSICA 14: £8
• *Tamara de Lempicka: Art Deco Icon*
The Sky in the Russian Landscape
by Alexander Pappaport
• *The Space of Russianness*
by Ekaterina Degot

**Rumiantsev's Ark: Library of a
Nation**
ROSSICA 12/13: £8
• Rumiantsev's Ark: Creation of the
National Russian Library
• Nikolai Fedorov: the Philosopher-
Librarian
• The Stalinist Leninka
• Tributes: Metropolitan Anthony of
Sourozh; John Stuart; Catherine Cooke

The Seductions of Europe
ROSSICA 5: £6
• Arkhangelskoe, the estate of
Prince Nikolai B. Yusupov, became a
sanctuary of Russian Enlightenment.
Prince Yusupov's collection rivalled
that of Catherine the Great.
• *Russian grand travellers in 18th-
century Europe* by Anthony Cross
• Dmitry Prigov's Phantom
Installations

**Moscow: the Third Rome,
Stalin's Capital, Global City**
ROSSICA 4: £6
• The Throne of Monomakh
• Moscow – New Jerusalem: Myth as
Reality
• A Vision of Paradise: Stalin's Moscow
• *Moscow as a Global City* by Catherine
Cooke

Imperial Russian Ballet
ROSSICA 3: £6
• Oranienbaum: Chinoiserie a la Russe
• Petipa and the Creation of Russian
Imperial Ballet
• Swan Lake: Lake of Tears
• The Chinese Palace at Oranienbaum,
Catherine the Great's Dacha

SUBSCRIBE TO ROSSICA

INTERNATIONAL REVIEW OF RUSSIAN CULTURE

ISSN 1472-9350

Rossica is a series of publications devoted to the many facets of Russian culture: past, present and future
Rossica is published by Academia Rossica, a non-profit organisation (UK Registered Charity no 1091022) created in 2000 with the aim of promoting a deeper international understanding of Russian culture.

UK subscription	Overseas subscription	Institutional subscription
4 issues: £40	4 issues: £50	4 issues: £75 (worldwide)
8 issues: £75	8 issues: £90	

I would like to subscribe to *Rossica* and/or order back issues

Name

Address

Postcode

Telephone   Email

Payment details

Please debit £   from my: ☐ Visa ☐ MasterCard ☐ Switch (please tick one)

Card no.   Security code

Expiry date   Issue no. (Switch only)

I enclose a cheque payable to 'Academia Rossica' for £

Gift Aid

If you are a UK tax-payer, please help us by giving your consent to reclaim tax on your subscription, increasing the value of your contribution by 28% at no extra cost to you.

I consent to Academia Rossica claiming Gift Aid on my contributions from 6 March 2011 until further notice.

Signature

Please send the completed form and payment to:
Academia Rossica, 76 Brewer Street, London W1F 9TX